D1083308

THE ONLY WOMAN IN THE ROOM

The author.

THE ONLY WOMAN IN THE ROOM

A MEMOIR

Beate Sirota Gordon

KODANSHA INTERNATIONAL
Tokyo • New York • London

ACKNOWLEDGMENTS

This autobiography was inspired by a video documentary of my life produced by Makiko Hiraoka of Akinori Suzuki's Osaka Documentary Workshop. I tape-recorded my story in Japanese and sent it to her for transcription. Using the tape as a basis, she gave it literary form in Japanese, and the book *1945 nen no Kurisumasu* (Kashiwashobo, 1995) was born. I thank her for her remarkable dedication. I am also indebted to Corinne Hoexter, who was the first to suggest that I write an autobiography.

My most profound thanks go to Stephen Shaw, chief editor at Kodansha International. Without Mr. Shaw's encouragement the task of creating this version would not have been undertaken. It was his sound advice that guided me in the changes I made. Arigato gozaimasu.

Distributed in the United States by Kodansha America, Inc., 114 Fifth Avenue, New York, N.Y. 10011, and in the United Kingdom and continental Europe by Kodansha Europe Ltd., 95 Aldwych, London WC2B 4JF. Published by Kodansha International Ltd., 17-14 Otowa 1-chome Bunkyo-ku, Tokyo 112, and Kodansha America, Inc. Copyright © 1997 by Beate Sirota Gordon. All rights reserved. Printed in Japan.
First edition, 1997
ISBN 4-7700-2145-3
97 98 99 00 9 8 7 6 5 4 3 2 1

CONTENTS

Homecoming

9

Vienna, My Birthplace

39

The House in Nogizaka

55

In Wartime America

75

The Equal Rights Clause

103

Career and Family

139

East and West

159

1

Homecoming

It was Christmas Eve, 1945.

As the propeller plane started its descent, I took out my compact and checked my reflection in the mirror. Although I had left New York more than two days before, there were no shadows under my eyes. I looked the way I felt, energetic and eager. Excitedly I applied lipstick and changed from summer clothes into a skirt and sweater, simultaneously praying and vowing as I did so: "Somehow I will find my mother and father."

The war had ended, but the thirty or so other passengers aboard the transport were all military men. Our flight from Guam had followed the route the B29 bombers used to take; after eight hours, we were finally approaching the coast of Japan. At the shoreline, the blue of the sea turned green where the waves broke in a swirl of lace. Beyond the beaches, farms and paddies came into view, arranged like so many playing cards, reminding me of the orderliness I had always associated with the Japanese. I was returning to Japan after an absence of five years. The dark green woods, gray-tiled roofs and narrow roads of the land I had longed to see again lay spread out below me. But then, after miles of fields and gardens, the scenery changed abruptly. Charred ruins and solitary chimneys stood up from the bare red earth like nails. This was the "land of the gods" that had once thought itself invincible. I had seen newspaper photos, of course, but the reality—especially from above—was utterly different. Soon we were at the outskirts of Yokohama. Atsugi Airport was close by, but the pilot deliberately circled for a while at low altitude, perhaps to show his passengers the sheer extent of the Allies' victory. It was an effective presentation. Looking down, I knew beyond a doubt that the Japanese were finished.

The soldiers on the plane whistled and flocked to the windows, exulting openly, but I felt numb with shock. We were all American citizens assigned to the General Headquarters of SCAP (Supreme Commander Allied Powers), where General Douglas MacArthur was directing the Occupation, but at that moment I was brought up short by the differences between us. To me, Japan meant home, the country where I had been brought up and where my parents still lived. Silently I said another prayer for their safety.

The plane banked away from Yokohama toward Atsugi Airport. Below us, I saw many other planes spread about, all American military aircraft, looking like great steel birds that had flown down to rest. A couple of them had red crosses on white backgrounds. Formerly a special base of the Imperial Japanese Navy, Atsugi now looked as if it had always been an American facility. Our transport continued to descend. On the ground several jeeps were moving about, and I caught glimpses of steel-helmeted soldiers and a single army tank. The soldiers on our plane had fallen silent, as though by agreement, and the cabin was filled with the noise of the engines. We touched down with a bump. The sun was already setting on this short winter's day.

We had flown from New York to the naval base at San Diego and from there to Hawaii. The next day brought us to tiny Johnston Island, then on to Guam and, at last, Atsugi. It was a trip of more than thirty hours.

It did not feel like Christmas Eve at Atsugi. A squad of soldiers appeared, marching back and forth, jeeps drove by, and fighter planes and transports were taking off and landing constantly. I could see Japanese men wearing white armbands and working under close supervision. It was apparent from their uniforms that they were former naval personnel, and their insignia showed high-ranking men among them. Presumably they still hadn't received permission to return to their families.

One of them caught my eye. Having grown up as a woman in Japan, I automatically looked down. But his response was to bow deeply. It seemed unthinkable: a Japanese serviceman deferring to me, a twenty-two-year-old Caucasian woman. For the second time I felt a stab of dismay at the totality of Japan's defeat.

There was already an immigration and customs office at Atsugi to deal with the numerous Allied personnel arriving there. Passport control was a formality. The soldier in charge merely looked at my photo, then at me, stamped "Occupied Japan" in my passport, thanked me and handed it back. He ignored the entries for my date of birth, birthplace (Vienna) and occupation. If he had checked the last, he would surely have questioned it. On my passport application I had written "research expert," but a State Department official had left out the word "research" and entered only "expert."

A jeep and driver were quickly found for me and my two suitcases, and we headed for Tokyo. Along the dusty road, all the signs were printed in English as well as Japanese. We passed through Yokohama, the damage caused by aerial bombardment—so dramatically visible from the plane—unfolding in scenes as still and silent as a frieze under the bleak December sky. What buildings had been left standing were smudged and blackened with smoke; not one of them had a pane of glass intact. Yet in the burned-out areas between the buildings rice had been planted, and the fragile green shoots of onions and winter radishes were visible amid the sea of red-brown rubble.

Night had fallen by the time we entered Tokyo. My heart was racing. As soon as I had learned that I would be returning to Japan, I had sent my parents a cable, so I hoped they would be waiting either at our house in Nogizaka or in the lobby of the Dai-Ichi Hotel in Shimbashi. We reached the Ginza. Shimbashi lay straight ahead, but first I had to leave my baggage at the billet assigned to me. Since I was the first civilian woman in occupied Japan, there was no separate billet for me; I had to stay with the WACS (Women's Army Corps) in one of the few buildings to have survived the fires. I left my bags in a room that housed six, and went off in the waiting jeep to the Dai-Ichi Hotel, which had been turned into living quarters for high-ranking GHQ officers. I pushed the front door open and entered eagerly.

The lobby was dark. I expected to hear my mother and father call my name, but apart from two naval officers, the place was deserted. I looked everywhere, even in the rest rooms, and inquired in vain at the reception desk for "a middle-aged European couple." At this point the two officers called out to me. They probably hadn't seen a young non-Asian woman in months, and wanted to know what the problem was.

"I was supposed to meet my parents here," I explained. "I sent a cable from New York." My voice rose sharply and wobbled.

"A cable?" one of the officers repeated, clearly amazed at my naïveté. "Haven't you seen the conditions here—after the bombing? Where did you send it? Isn't it obvious that a cable can't be delivered?"

The other man saw that I was near tears.

"What are your parents' names?" he asked kindly.

I told him their names and my father's profession—pianist—but I felt devastated. The possibility that the cable hadn't been delivered had never crossed my mind.

"Leo Sirota? Someone as famous as that shouldn't be hard to find." These encouraging words from the direction of the reception desk did not register at first. My thoughts were filled with the recent memory of blood-colored rubble. How in the world was I going to find my parents in the midst of all that? I couldn't stop crying. The only thing that gave me hope was the fact that two months earlier, in mid-October, I had been informed by a *Time* magazine correspondent that he had met my parents in Karuizawa. Common sense told me they must still be alive.

"I know about your father," the young woman at the reception desk said in English, coming over.

"You know him?" I exclaimed, automatically speaking in Japanese for the first time since coming back. "Have you seen him?"

The woman stared at me in surprise.

"You speak Japanese very well," she said, forgetting my distress.

"Have you seen him?" I pressed.

"I heard him in a concert on the radio yesterday," she told me, collecting herself.

It must have been a live performance, since there were no tape recordings at that time. Impulsively, I called JOAK, the main broadcasting station, and learned that my father had in fact left for Karuizawa, some five hours north of Tokyo, early that morning. They were kind enough to give me the address, which I recognized immediately—it was our summer house. With the reassurance that my parents were alive, my spirits lifted. I asked the receptionist at the hotel to send a telegram, which read simply: "I am waiting for you at the Dai-Ichi Hotel in Shimbashi. Kisses, Beate."

The officers were still sitting there.

"Are you in the armed forces?" they wanted to know.

"I'm an American civilian," I said.

"How did you manage to get here as a civilian?" one of them asked.

The other interrupted him before I could reply.

"You must have come as an interpreter. Your Japanese is so good."

"I lived in Tokyo as a little girl," I explained, "so I picked it up then. I wanted to see my parents again, and ordinary civilians aren't allowed in Japan, so I found a job as a civilian attached to the army, and that's how I got back home to Japan."

The two men showed no reaction when I described Japan as "home," and did not quiz me any further. Having come to Tokyo directly from the battlefield, they wanted to hear news of *their* home, so they persuaded me to sit down with them by ordering me a hot chocolate. As a newcomer to war-ravaged Japan, I didn't realize how precious a thing like that was, but the steaming drink did help remind me that it was Christmas.

The next day, I decided to try to find our old house in Tokyo, which meant going to the motor pool for a jeep and driver. Buses and streetcars were off-limits to Allied personnel, to prevent putting further strain on already overtaxed Japanese facilities. I asked the driver in Japanese to take me to Nogizaka, the Tokyo neighborhood around Nogi Shrine where my family had lived before the war.

The man sat up, startled.

"Where did you learn Japanese?" he asked.

"I was brought up in Japan from the age of five to fifteen—in Tokyo." It was dawning on me that this was a story I would be telling often.

"Are your parents American?"

"They're Austrians of Russian origin, and I was born in Vienna."

"Why did you come to Japan?" was the next question.

"My father is a musician, Leo Sirota, the pianist. He's well known here."

"So," he said, sitting back, "you're the daughter of a musician."

The driver continued to ply me with questions, but as we approached the central areas where fires had raged he fell silent. Even here, however, there were signs of revival. The Hibiya streetcar, whose route followed the Imperial Palace moat, was already running again. The passing streetcars were all overcrowded, with people clinging on, front and back. Seeing young women with babies strapped to their backs hanging on to the doors, I couldn't help crying out in Japanese, "That's dangerous!" The babies' cold-nipped feet, dangling from quilted jackets, were as red as persimmons. When the jeep passed the Diet building, I noticed that the vast, empty area in front of it was being cultivated, with wheat and vegetables planted in rows.

But when we neared my old neighborhood, the atmosphere changed. There were a few buildings left standing, but I could see no private homes. Everything I remembered had vanished. Only the dark green woods of Nogi Shrine, rising out of the now familiar reddish-brown surroundings, appeared untouched.

"My house is very near here," I told the driver.

I got out at Nogi Shrine and just stood there for two or three minutes, looking down the hill in confusion. If one walks down the hill, the shrine is on the left. Past the shrine, there had been houses on the right. Now the houses were simply gone. What I saw was utterly changed from what I remembered. Even so, I kept looking.

"No. 10 Hinokicho, Akasaka-ku, Tokyo." I murmured the address to myself as I walked down Nogizaka Hill searching for the Western-style house in which I had lived for ten years. The houses of our neighbors— the singer Nobuko Hara, the Chinese consul, the White Russian, the German—had all been destroyed. Nor was our house where my feet told me it should be. What I was looking at were merely traces of it, the square foundation stones. My eyes swam, and the rust-colored mounds of earth became swollen and distorted. In the end, I was only able to recognize the remains of the house from a stone pillar, now scorched by flames, one of two that used to stand next to the front steps. A chill ran through me. The war had damaged not just stones and mortar but the very stuff of people's memories. Where was my friend's house? Was the street that led to the school still there? What about the storekeeper?

Trying to revive my fast-fading and by now thoroughly disoriented recollections, I rode around in the jeep for a long time. Finally, I came across the house of a German singer we had known, a Mrs. Netke, and knocked at the cracked glass door.

"This is Beate Sirota," I shouted in German.

Pale and thin, Mrs. Netke very cautiously opened the door and stuck her head out. When she saw me, a look of recognition lit up her watery blue eyes.

"Your parents are probably in Karuizawa," she told me. "During the war, all the foreigners living in Tokyo, even those from the Axis countries, had to go there."

The morning's grim sights had made me briefly forget last night's telegram to my parents. Mrs. Netke's words jolted me back into the present, and I was suddenly anxious to return to the Dai-Ichi Hotel in case news had come. Although she was eager to talk about the past, I hastily said goodbye and jumped into the jeep.

There was nothing new at the hotel, however. The postal service was in such disarray that there was no way of knowing whether my telegram had even arrived. The two naval officers were sitting together in the same place in the lobby, so we picked up where we had left off, chatting about New York. But while I was regaling them with accounts of the latest concerts and movies, I was privately calculating how long it would take for my parents to reach Tokyo if they had received my telegram. The trains ran so infrequently they might not arrive until evening. After a while, I couldn't hide my preoccupation any longer. To cheer me up, the officers invited me to visit their ship, which was lying at anchor in Tokyo Bay. Even after fifty years, I have not forgotten the laughing, sweating faces of the sailors or the strange metallic beauty of the ship's cannons, which I knew must have been used to fire on Japanese.

By 5:30 I was back in the hotel.

"Beate!"

It took me a moment to recognize my father. He was wearing an old black cashmere coat that I remembered, but his cheeks were hollow and his face was deeply lined. Only his voice was the same. He hugged me hard and kissed my cheek.

"How is Mama?" I asked him anxiously.

"She's ill," he admitted. "She's suffering from malnutrition, which is why she couldn't come. But don't worry. When she sees your face, she'll get better in no time." When my father smiled his wrinkles deepened, and he looked much older than his sixty years. But his eyes still twinkled.

We sat there holding hands and talking. Each of us had painful wartime stories to tell. My father dwelt in particular on the fate of his relatives in Europe. The Sirotas, like my mother's family, the Horensteins, were Russian Jews. Between the two families, there were dozens of relatives in Austria, Switzerland, France and the Soviet Union. My mother was one of sixteen children; her father had been widowed twice and married three times. My father had four brothers and sisters. His younger brother, Peter, Maurice Chevalier's agent, had been living in Vichy France but was arrested by the Nazis and sent to Auschwitz. Luckily,

Peter's daughter Tina escaped. My father's nephew Igor was killed in the Normandy Invasion, and my mother's nephew Josef, who lived in Switzerland, had been reported safe. But the relatives living in Austria had all been deported to Nazi camps. Whenever the words "concentration camp" came up, the lines in my father's face seemed to grow even deeper.

As we were talking, the chandelier lights suddenly went out.

"That's the second time today," a voice in the lobby said.

I held my father's hands tightly until the lights came on again. His strong pianist's fingers felt as bony and rough as a tree's branches, but their warmth was reassuring.

We talked for hours, but finally I had to return to the WAC billet. My father stayed overnight with one of his pupils, whose house had escaped the fire-bombing, and set off alone the next day for Karuizawa. I had to start work, but I promised to follow him to Karuizawa as soon as I could.

The next morning I reported to GHQ. In Washington I had been told only that I would be working for the Government Section of SCAP in Tokyo, so I had no idea what the job entailed. On that first day, I was interviewed by the deputy chief of the Government Section, Colonel Charles L. Kades, who decided to assign me to the Political Affairs Division, headed by Colonel Pieter K. Roest. I was embarrassed to have to ask my superior for a favor so soon. If I had been working for the Japanese, I would have hemmed and hawed, but this was an American world. When I explained my parents' situation to Col. Roest, he quickly granted me leave.

The electric lamps at Karuizawa Station shed a faint, blurred light when I stepped off the train. I was more than cold: I felt as if I were being stung by a thousand icy needles. As a child, I used to go to Karuizawa every summer with my parents, but I had never been there in the winter before. When I saw the lights of our cottage, though, I forgot the cold. "Mama!" I cried, and started running. My father met me at the door and I ran straight upstairs to my parents' bedroom. My mother lay on a wooden bed, her face pale and puffy. I was struck by the fact that even in this condition she had put her hair up.

"Mama…" I burst into tears. I couldn't speak.

"Beate, Beate, my Beate," she repeated, patting my back and stroking my hair, just as she had done when I was a child after having a bad dream.

Instead of her familiar sweet smell, there was a sour odor, reminding me that she was ill. Malnutrition had reduced my father's body to skin and bone, while my mother's was visibly swollen.

"Beate, I have something to show you. Lend me your shoulder." Holding on to me, my mother slowly got up and led me into the next room. On the desk was a pile of colorful packages, some tied with ribbons.

"These are belated birthday and Christmas presents," she said. "After the war started and we couldn't send anything abroad, we set them aside for you." There were five years' worth of presents dating back to 1941. I hugged her.

"Your mother always prayed that she could give you these things in person," my father said, putting his arms around our shoulders. The heap of presents brought back memories of lonely birthdays and holidays in America. Although there had been no bombs falling there, life on my own had sometimes been a struggle.

When I unwrapped the packages, I found feather-light silk material, a pearl necklace and an amethyst brooch. I learned later that my mother had exchanged some jewels of her own for these beautiful things. I brought my parents chocolate bars and perfume from the Army PX on the Ginza, as well as some cookies my WAC roommate had given me.

At our family reunion that evening, tea and milk played a central role. My mother had saved some evaporated milk in anticipation of this day. We sat there enjoying the warmth of the teacups and beaming at each other. Relief was the main course. With half a decade to talk about, we hardly knew where to begin. Everything seemed important. But the questions soon flowed: How did you pay your tuition when no money came from us? What kind of work did you do to pay your expenses? How hard was it getting back to Japan? And they too began to describe their years of isolation, confined to a small country town in Japan.

The winters had been particularly tough. The summer house was not insulated, and it was incredibly drafty. My parents had only one stove downstairs and a couple of small kerosene heaters upstairs. The walls were cracked, and in midwinter the floors became slippery with ice. My mother told me that an egg left overnight on the kitchen table would freeze so hard you could throw it on the floor and it wouldn't break. The water pipes had occasionally burst at night and turned the kitchen floor into a skating rink.

During the war years, the little community of foreigners had helped each other in the annual struggle against the cold. One New Year's Eve, a neighbor gave a "hot bath party." (My father interrupted the story to recall how, when he first came to Japan in 1928 and didn't know the customs of the country, he went into the bathroom at the inn where he was staying. Seeing a gentleman and two ladies in the large tub, he quickly retreated, but the man called after him, "Come in, come in, it's only my wife and daughter.") Resuming her tale, my mother recalled how their neighbor, having enough fuel on this occasion to heat water for his big bathtub, had invited all his guests to take a Japanese-style bath—that is, wash and rinse oneself outside the bath and then duck into it for a warm soak. My mother had the honor of being the first in.

She also told me about a friend's family whose four children all had dysentery at the same time. There wasn't enough food for them, and their governess came to my mother begging for anything she could spare—the children would die, she said, unless they got something to eat. My mother gave them her entire ration of potatoes, all the food she had, and the children survived. She told me, too, what happened when one of my father's pupils heard that an eruption of the nearby volcano, Mt. Asama, had shattered all the windows in my parents' cottage. Japanese were forbidden to associate with them, yet this young woman traveled four hours by train from Tokyo, carrying glass for the windows, and installed it with the help of her mother, who had accompanied her on the long, risky journey. Also, once in a while my mother would find a package of food at the front door, left by some courageous Japanese friend in the middle of the night...

At some point in all this, my father said: "Beate, you must be tired. I think you should go to bed."

As he spoke, I realized how the long day's accumulated fatigue had worn me down, so I followed his advice. But the bed was icy. Even with all my clothes on, I couldn't sleep, and my head was spinning.

"Beate, are you cold?" my mother called out. Although she could barely walk, she brought me three woolen blankets and also put my father's coat over me.

Snug in this cocoon, I eventually fell asleep.

I had been given three days off from GHQ. During this time I had to get my frail parents moved from Karuizawa to Tokyo, a five-hour trip by car, so the next day saw a burst of activity as we got things packed and ready.

But there was nowhere to go. Even if one were willing to pay for a hotel in Tokyo, all the places that had not burned down had been commandeered by the Allies. There simply was no lodging available for civilians.

I had been moved from the WAC billet to Kanda Kaikan, the former YMCA headquarters. Because I did not want my mother to be left alone when my father had to travel for concerts, I asked permission for her to stay there with me. Permission was refused.

The only remaining option was to turn to my father's students. Many had been wealthy before the war, but in the disorder and destruction of the intervening years he had lost contact with them. The only one he was still in touch with was Shigeko Kaneko, in whose house he had stayed on the night of our reunion in Tokyo. Fortunately, my parents were now able to rent two rooms in her house.

The next requirement was medical care. Finding a doctor was simple, but getting a consultation was not. The doctor recommended by Miss Kaneko responded after two calls, but stipulated that he be paid in food. He himself had to give food in order to obtain medicine, we were told.

With supplies severely reduced, the Japanese—more than seventy million of them—were starving. Food-related incidents were common. A mother and daughter trying to steal vegetables in a field were killed by an electric fence. A Tokyo judge died of malnutrition rather than buy food on the black market. People were sentenced to quite long terms in jail for stealing sweet potatoes. Even for me, a member of GHQ and on the winning side, it was a problem getting extra food. I had plenty to eat myself at my billet, but finding food for my parents was a formidable task, let alone finding enough to barter for medical care. The seven bars of Hershey's chocolate I had taken to Karuizawa represented a week's ration. Within hours, my mother had traded them for enough rice and eggs to last many days.

In the end, the rescue operation for my parents turned out fairly well. They were under the care of the hungry Japanese doctor for a while, but eventually I was able to arrange for them to go to the U.S. Army clinic, where they were given essential vitamins. In time, they began to recover. More important still, we were together again.

Each morning, I walked from the Kanda Kaikan to work, a twenty-five-minute walk along the Imperial Palace moat. Of all the buildings still standing in Tokyo in 1945, the one belonging to the Dai-Ichi Insurance Company, opposite the vast grounds of the palace, was perhaps the most imposing. This was the building SCAP had designated as its headquarters. I would go in through the grand main entrance and lobby, with its lofty ceiling and massive pillars, to reach the elevators for the Government Section offices on the sixth floor. With the office of the Supreme Commander on the same floor, this was the heart of GHQ.

I was afraid of General MacArthur and used to hide behind a pillar when he passed by. I was also too much in awe of the head of our section, General Courtney Whitney, ever to take him up on something I remember him telling us on New Year's Eve:

"I want your reaction to every directive to the Japanese government prepared in this section. The junior officers are as well, if not better, qualified to pass judgment on our moves as the higher-ranking ones, including myself. I mean exactly as I say. And I look forward to the time when a lieutenant will barge into my office, bang on my desk and say, 'Goddammit, general, such-and-such a proposed directive is preposterous, and you'd be out of your mind to ask General MacArthur to approve it.'"

The Government Section was by and large a group of legal scholars and professors-in-uniform. Most were believers in President Roosevelt's New Deal; all were enthusiastic about instituting what they saw as much-needed reforms in Japan. Gen. Whitney, who was so close to MacArthur that even their handwriting was similar, and who spent an hour or two every day closeted with him, had been his lawyer in Manila. The deputy chief, Col. Kades, had been a counsel to the federal government. Kades's roots were in a town in Spain near the border with France, and, like me, he was Jewish. He had served in Europe and found himself stationed in France at the end of the war. At just over forty, he was in his prime; with a sharp mind, a cool manner and a gift for leadership, he also had extraordinary charm. Being young, I particularly appreciated the way he explained things in a friendly fashion without being patronizing. Even the most obtuse questions failed to strain his patience. Only one thing about him disturbed me. Near his desk, along with a sign bearing the Chinese characters for democracy, he had placed a bamboo sword that had been used by the secret police to torture people. Although I admired the colonel, I questioned his judgment in using such a potent symbol of Japan's former tyranny as an ornament.

The Political Affairs Division to which I had been assigned consisted of Col. Pieter K. Roest, aged forty-seven; Dr. Harry Emerson Wildes, the oldest member of the Government Section at fifty-five; and myself, aged twenty-two. Roest, born in Holland, had been an anthropologist before the war, studying the caste system in India and traveling widely in other parts of Asia and the Middle East. Although a lot of people in the section kept their distance from him, considering his vegetarianism and early advocacy of alternative medicine eccentric, I was sympathetic to him, in part because I got to like his beautiful, gentle young wife. She was a WAC and also worked in GHQ, which had few married couples in it.

Dr. Wildes, an economist who had taught at Keio University from 1924 to 1925, was a rather mercurial character, but because of the research he had done in prewar Japan, he was probably more familiar with Japanese customs than anyone else in the section except me. His interest and knowledge, despite an inadequate grasp of the language, gave us something in common.

We were an unusual trio, but we worked together well.

"Beate, you grew up in Japan and your Japanese is fluent," Col. Roest had said aloud while reading my résumé on my first day there in late December.

"What other languages do you speak?" Dr. Wildes asked.

"I was born in Vienna and went to a German school as a little girl in Japan, so I know German. I learned French and Russian from a tutor. And I learned Spanish in America, in college."

Wildes nodded and looked at Roest.

"So, when you add English and Japanese, you've got six languages," he said. "Colonel, we have a language expert here."

This established my "credentials," but I still had a lot to learn. I understood that our primary concern was to study Japan's political parties, as the foundation stones of the country's democratization, and that for democracy to prevail the Occupation authorities would have to purge from government all nationalists who had been active in the militarist era. I also understood the logic behind the particular assignment I was given: the study of women in politics, since I was a woman, and the status of minor political parties, since I was the least experienced member of the group. But I needed to know more of the background of Occupation policy.

Patiently, they explained the key developments in the months since August 30, 1945, when MacArthur had landed in his private plane, the *Bataan*, from Manila by way of Okinawa. Gen. Whitney, traveling with him, had taken notes of his directives on Japan: "First destroy the military... Then build the structure of representative government... Enfranchise the women... Free the political prisoners... Liberate the farmers... Establish a free labor movement... Encourage a free economy... Abolish police oppression... Develop a free and responsible press... Liberalize education... Decentralize political power..."

The Allies had not expected the degree of compliance they actually encountered. I remembered hearing in New York that a group of zealous young soldiers opposed to the Emperor's decision to surrender had staged a coup d'etat in the neighborhood of the Imperial Palace and at Atsugi Airport. The coup failed, and the soldiers committed ritual suicide in front of the palace. Even worse, on the day the war ended, a special attack wing of the Japanese air force had taken off from an airfield in Kyushu. No one returned.

By the end of August, however, the Allies met with absolutely no resistance, either on land or at sea, and the plan to administer military government directly was dropped in favor of a system of indirect administration through the Japanese government. The Japanese were in no doubt, though, that it was MacArthur and—behind him—America's Initial Post-Surrender Policy, as applied by three key sections of GHQ (Government; Economic and Scientific; Civil Information and Education), that were in control of their country.

Steps were quickly taken to round up prominent militarists and to suppress any future possibility of a military revival. Tojo, prime minister at the outset of the war, was arrested with a number of other Class A war criminals and imprisoned in Sugamo. Censorship of newspapers and other publications, broadcasts, movies and mail was instituted.

Drawing immediate criticism from *The New York Times* and the *New York Herald Tribune*, MacArthur appointed Prince Fumimaro Konoe, a prewar prime minister and an intimate of the imperial family, to lead a group of Japanese constitutional experts to revise the existing constitution. The group had already started work when Konoe killed himself with poison in mid-December.

A day later, the Lower House, prodded by SCAP, promulgated the revised election law, and women's suffrage became a reality. And in the first week of January 1946, a widespread purge of rightists in responsible positions, including people in the fields of finance, commerce and agriculture, was announced.

Mesmerized by the steady clacking of my typewriter, my head bent over the keys, I was always surprised to find when I looked up that it was five o'clock and time to go back to the Kanda Kaikan for dinner. There were often incidents on the way. My route took me past some U.S. Army billets, and even though it was winter, the windows would open and whistles rain down like a summer shower. There were two hundred thousand Allied personnel stationed in Japan, and only sixty of them were women: a ratio of over three thousand to one. To the GIs, I suppose, I was the embodiment of the women back home. On Saturdays, I was overwhelmed with requests for dates. I found it impossible to tell whether these men were really interested in me or simply trying to pick up an unattached American woman, so I made a point of ignoring most of them.

I was not against dating on principle, though. It was, after all, a way of getting those precious Hershey bars at the PX.

"If you like chocolate so much, why don't you eat it?" my date would ask.

"I'm full," I'd say. "I'll eat it tonight, while I'm reading. That's what I like to do."

But there was one man who was more perceptive.

"I brought you some chocolate last time," he said. "Did you sell it to someone? Do you need money?"

Navy Lieutenant Warren Brown had evidently noticed how carefully I'd stored the chocolate bars away in my bag.

"I'm sorry," I confessed. "My parents are ill, and I give them the bars so they can trade them for butter and eggs."

"They must be in bad shape," he said. "I've heard that the foreigners who were here during the war had a terrible time."

He offered to give me his PX card. I refused it, but I was grateful.

One day the following week, he called me.

"Let's meet in front of the Dai-Ichi Building tonight at 5:30," he said. "I'll pick you up. I'll be driving."

His voice at the other end of the line sounded tense. As arranged, I waited under the watchful eyes of the military policemen stationed in front of the building. At the appointed time, Lt. Brown arrived driving a weapons carrier, which was much larger than his usual jeep. I pretended not to notice that he looked a lot less relaxed than usual as he gripped the steering wheel. He spoke without looking at me.

"I'd like you to introduce me to your parents."

We had only met a few times, and I thought his suggestion a bit premature, but seeing his determined expression I agreed.

We headed for my parents' rented quarters. When I spoke to him during the trip he listened absentmindedly. I thought he was concentrating on driving because he wasn't used to the truck. In the rearview mirror he noticed a large military vehicle closing in on us. He maintained his speed, but his jaw tightened. The soldiers in the truck glanced at the two of us, grinned, and passed by. He gave a sigh of relief. When we came to the intersection near my parents' house we found three MPs stationed there. Lt. Brown's color changed; his face twitched, and although it was the dead of winter, he was sweating. I suppressed the urge to ask him questions. The MPs made no move to stop us.

When we reached the Kaneko house where my parents were staying, my mother came out leaning on my father's arm. Lt. Brown whipped the canvas off the rear of the truck like a bullfighter flourishing his cape.

"Navy food isn't that great," he said to them, "but I've brought you a few cases of it."

The "few cases" turned out to be four wooden boxes containing beef, butter, jam, sardines, sugar, ice-cream powder and chocolate.

"Lieutenant…," I said, and stopped, unable to go on.

This Santa Claus had brought not only foodstuffs but bars of Lux soap. My mother closed her eyes.

"I haven't had any cosmetic soap for years, I've been using laundry soap," she murmured. "What a lovely smell!"

Even though American troops were given abundant amounts of food to eat, it was almost impossible to lay in a large supply of anything. Lt. Brown told us not to worry; it was surplus stuff he'd been ordered to destroy. I shivered when I realized that if the MPs had found out about it, I, too, would have been hauled before a military court. Thanks to this food, however, my mother's pale, puffy body soon returned to normal. My father's skin, which was wrinkled like old paper, filled out. I saw this officer a few more times, but before long he received new orders and said goodbye. He had just turned twenty-five.

I consoled myself by going to parties. One particularly memorable party took place in the Imperial Hotel. Russia's chief representative in Japan, General Derevyanko, was entertaining a high Occupation official, General Marquat, whose secretary, Virginia, was a former roommate of mine. She invited me because I was the only female member of the American contingent who spoke Russian.

The suite was enormous—five or six connecting rooms—and the tables were laid out end to end in a line. As the lowest in rank, I sat at the end of the last table, right up against a sink.

I am not much of a drinker, so when the vodka toasts began I was alarmed. One planter's punch or a frozen daiquiri keeps me happy all evening, so several straight shots of vodka in succession would be far too much. What to do? I leaned back in my chair and felt for the edge of the sink. At the next toast, I took my glass and, without turning around, surreptitiously poured it away. I went through at least eight toasts like this, and was thinking how clever I was when the host's aide-de-camp came over with a bottle of white wine and said, "Maybe you'd like this better."

When dinner was over, Gen. Derevyanko, who had not poured his vodka down the sink, put one arm around my waist and the other around Virginia's and carried us into the next room. Although we were both slim, I was astonished that he could carry both of us.

It was easy at the time to underestimate the importance of women's suffrage. Japanese women had had to endure the loss of husbands, sons and homes and the horror of the air raids. War was a huge price to pay for getting the vote. Indeed, barely subsisting now amid the ruins of their lives, how could they be expected to pay attention to "suffrage"? For most of them, it must have seemed a very abstract notion. To tell the truth, I myself had never voted up to then.

With these thoughts turning over in my mind, I went one day to visit my parents. Just as I reached their house, I saw a woman pulling a cart loaded with pots, in one of which some rice was cooking. She was wearing an air-raid helmet of the kind that had been used in the war by the Civilian Defense Corps for protection during the bombings. Now the helmet was lined with cotton to keep out the cold. The child she was carrying on her back wore a similar helmet. The woman lifted her head and looked at me.

"Miss Beate!" she exclaimed.

It was Mio Sawabe, who had worked in our Nogizaka house for eight years.

"Mio-san, Mio-san!" I cried, embracing her. "How did you find us?"

"I searched," she said simply. "In fact, I went to Karuizawa to find out where you all were."

"All the way to Karuizawa?" I was amazed.

"All through the war, I worried about your parents," she told me. "I thought they'd have trouble getting food. I wanted to bring them something, but the police were always watching…"

She began to cry, remembering the past, and then laughed so loudly about our unexpected reunion in the street that my parents came out of the house.

"I *thought* it was you, Mio-san," my mother said.

"Just wait a minute," she told us, "—I'm cooking some rice."

Letting the child down from the harness on her back, she took the pots from the cart and checked the fire. She'd brought a plateful of dried fish from her house near Numazu, just as she used to do in the old days. She was wearing workman's clothes and looked as poised, strong and capable as ever.

"It's so wonderful that you're alive!" I told her.

"I don't know whether it's better to be alive or dead," she answered, her voice turning grim for a moment. "I guess living is better."

The rice was ready. In those days it was usually mixed with some filler like potato, radish or bamboo and cooked with a lot of water to make a mush that could be called "rice" only as a courtesy. That was what most families ate. But this was pure. My mother brought out the butter Lt. Brown had given us, and the piping hot rice glistened.

"Ah, the smell of rice and butter," said my mother.

Sniffing the steam rising from the rice, Mio-san nodded. My father, eating a mouthful, sighed.

My thoughts about elections and suffrage were forgotten amid the sensations of this once everyday delight. Women's rights were a necessity, I knew, but they were a luxury, too, in a land without enough rice or butter.

My maternal grandmother, Bertha, in 1899.

My maternal stepgrandmother, Marie, in 1902.

My mother, Augustine (Gisa) Horenstein, aged eighteen, in Vienna.

My mother and her brother Jascha, the conductor, in 1917.

There were rumors that my mother posed nude for this portrait, which appeared on the cover of a Viennese fashion magazine.

My father, Leo Sirota, in Kiev, aged eleven.

Leo in St. Petersburg, 1901.

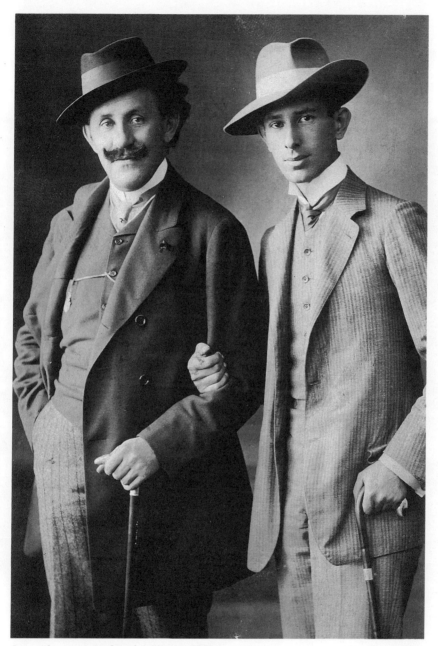

Leo with a musician friend in Vienna, 1908.

My father's trio: Robert Pollak (violin) and Friedrich Buxbaum (cello), in Vienna, 1927.

2

Vienna, My Birthplace

"Please don't ever stay away so long again." My mother's voice qua-vered. She held my father's hand in both of hers as she spoke, and then kissed it.

It was 1928, the evening of his return from a year-long concert tour with the pianist Egon Petri. I was five years old. My father and Petri had been touring the industrial cities of the Ukraine and had met with such success that the tour was extended several times. After five nights of recitals in Vladivostok, on the east coast of Russia, my father had also been asked to perform in northeast China. The puppet state of Man-chukuo had not yet been established, but the Japanese had taken over the South Manchurian Railway.

"The local officials prepared a special train for me, decorated with branches of green leaves, garlands of flowers and ribbons," he told us. "It was quite embarrassing. But the best thing was that on a little platform in the club car they'd put a piano—a genuine Steinway. At several stops I gave concerts on it. The sides of the car opened out, and the audience stood around it."

He performed in various cities on his journey across Manchuria before reaching Harbin, the capital, which to him had a noticeably Russian atmosphere. There had been a Russian concession in the city since 1896, and many White Russians had fled there after the revolution in 1917. He gave eight concerts with eight different programs in Harbin; all were sold out several days in advance. Stravinsky's *Petrushka* was particularly popular, it seemed.

After the Stravinsky, a Japanese gentleman named Kosaku Yamada came to see him at the Hotel Moderne. Yamada, a great admirer of avant-garde Russian music, asked him if he would consider giving a series of recitals in Japan. The terms he offered were generous, and my father, having already come that far, felt he might as well continue.

He was greatly impressed by the scenery he traveled through in Japan. Once, from the train window, he saw Mt. Fuji, with its snow-capped summit. "You'd never forget it—it's superb," he told us, describing the shape of the mountain with his hands. "I hope you two will see it someday."

The audiences at his performances in Japan—one every other day, sixteen in all—"went crazy," as he put it, and the reviews were equally flattering. "It's hard to imagine," he said, "but the Japanese treat an artist they like as if he were a king. They're sophisticated, too—their history and culture are comparable, after all, to our own. Japan's going to be a great country one day."

Then he dropped his bombshell.

"Mr. Yamada invited me to go there and teach. They've offered me a position as professor of music at the Imperial Academy. Also, I can give concerts whenever it suits me. They want me for at least half a year."

Despite his enthusiasm, he was watching my mother's reaction closely. Her face clouded over.

"Don't leave us on our own again," she said, shaking her head. He could hear the note of desperate protest in her voice.

Their conversation continued, but my nanny shepherded me off to bed, and though I really would have liked to stay there with my father, I also wanted to show him I knew enough to understand that he wished to be alone with my mother. It was dark in the bedroom, but I was excited and had a hard time falling asleep. From my room, which was separated from the living room by a hallway, I was unable to hear what they were saying.

My father, Leo Sirota, was born into a Jewish family in Kiev on May 4, 1885. His father had been in the dry-goods business. Leo, the fourth of five children, grew up in an artistic atmosphere. Renting a room in their house was the pianist Michael Winkler, and whenever Winkler played, my father managed to station himself nearby. When Leo was five, Winkler invited his young listener to take lessons from him. He was astonished by the boy's abilities. "This child has talent," he told Leo's father.

When he was nine, Leo gave his first recital, and in the same year he entered the Imperial Music School in Kiev. Among his classmates was Sergei Tarnowski, who would later become Vladimir Horowitz's teacher. At ten, he went on his first Russian concert tour. Paderewski heard him play and invited him to come to Paris and study with him, but Leo's mother, thinking the boy was too young, rejected the idea. When he was eleven, though, he started giving lessons himself. On snowy days, the Sirotas' maid would take him by the hand and escort him to the home of his student, who was nine years older than he was.

Leo was a fun-loving child. He kept a dozen pigeons which accompanied him to school every day and then flew home. His position among the other boys in the Gymnasium was secure, apparently, because his best friend was the class bully, whom Leo helped with his mathematics and who, in return, wouldn't let anyone touch a hair on his head. Another friend was the son of a rich Kiev merchant, who traded his black caviar sandwiches for Leo's more modest lunch because he was "tired" of caviar. The lifelong taste for caviar that he acquired as a result was later passed on to me.

At fourteen he became the head music coach of the Kiev State Opera. On one occasion he even accompanied the great singer Fyodor Chaliapin. After graduating from the Imperial Music School, he went to St. Petersburg, where he was awarded the Artist's Diploma at the Conservatory. Its director, the composer Alexander Glazunov, then wrote a letter of recommendation for him to Ferruccio Busoni, the Italian composer-pianist who was teaching in Vienna at the time and was on friendly terms with both Mahler and Sibelius. A proponent of the new harmony, Busoni played a leading role in trying to fuse the old and the new in music.

In July 1904, the Russian minister for interior affairs was assassinated, and riots ensued. The dissatisfaction of the Russian public was directed not only against soldiers and politicians, but against Jews. Leo now had various incentives to leave Russia. Besides the groundswell of anti-Semitism in his homeland, there was the example of two of his siblings, already living in Paris and Warsaw respectively. To his parents, the departure of their fourth child for Vienna in 1904 must have come as no great surprise.

Turn-of-the-century Vienna, capital of the Austro-Hungarian Empire, had almost two million inhabitants. An extraordinary zest characterized the city in its imperial twilight. Streetcars, which had been running for just two years, jostled the horse-drawn carriages of the wealthy. Children squealed in the famous Prater amusement park. Students sat around in "bohemian" cafés, and the Paris, Berlin and London newspapers were widely read. It was a truly cosmopolitan city.

For a talented, good-looking and *simpatico* young man like Leo, social opportunities abounded, and he found himself surrounded by women. He was invited to salons, frequented the Freudenau racecourse outside the city and attended society balls. In her will, one of his rich Viennese fans left him a small apartment house. To the Viennese, beauty was a kind of nobility, art commanded respect, and pleasure, it was believed, was the wellspring of art. There was a brilliant shimmer to the city in those years of decline. Nineteen-year-old Leo was captivated. Home, by contrast, meant the anxieties and privations of the ongoing Russo-Japanese War.

Leo, deciding not to use his letter of introduction to Busoni immediately but to choose a teacher for himself, attended classes given by Josef Hoffman, Leopold Godowsky, Ignace Paderewski and Busoni. He auditioned for each of them, and all four accepted him; only then did he choose the Italian. When Leo gave him the letter from Glazunov, he responded, smiling: "What need is there for this? I have heard you play!"

Four years later, at a lesson, Leo played Liszt's "Don Juan Fantasy." At first his teacher was silent. Then he strode to the piano and closed the lid.

"After that masterful piece of playing," he said, "I don't wish to hear anyone else today." He then went to his desk, took out a copy of his own composition, *Elegien*, and inscribed on it: "To my young colleague from Kiev, for the 'Don Juan Fantasy' on May 4, 1908, in Vienna. Cordially, Ferruccio Busoni." It was Leo's twenty-third birthday. He always prized this dedication for that one word, "colleague." Later, Busoni would also dedicate his Giga, Bolero e Variazione, a study after Mozart, "to Leo."

It was a time of intense musical activity in Vienna, and aspiring pianists sought recognition in various competitions. Artur Rubinstein, who became a lifelong friend, has recorded his memories of one such contest: "None of [my] pieces was really ready for a competition. I was always able to give them a musically fine outline, but I neglected detail and technical finish, a vice which lasted for many years... On the third day of the competition, Edwin Fischer was again the first to play... After Fischer, I heard Sirota, Pyshnov and an Englishman. They depressed me—they played too well. All four had the kind of technical polish which I never possessed, and they never missed a note—the devils."*

In 1910 an event that attracted the interest of all musical Europe catapulted Leo Sirota to fame. On December 18 Busoni conducted the Tonkünstler Orchestra in a program that included the "Don Juan Fantasy" and Mozart's Sonata in D for two pianos, with Busoni and Sirota performing. The pièce de résistance, however, was the premiere of Busoni's Concerto for Piano, Orchestra and Chorus, with my father as soloist. There were sixteen curtain calls. Leo was just twenty-five years old.

Busoni predicted a glittering future for his protégé. The road ahead seemed smooth and straight. But in June 1914 the Austrian Archduke Franz Ferdinand was assassinated in Sarajevo, and by August all of Europe was at war. Suddenly, nobody's future was predictable.

My father was luckier than most. As a Russian citizen, he escaped Austrian military service and was able to continue studying music with Busoni as well as taking classes in philosophy, law and music history at the University of Vienna. On Sundays, he played for Jascha Horenstein, another native of Kiev, who practiced his conducting skills with a "pick-up" orchestra. Horenstein, later to become internationally renowned for his interpretations of Mahler, had no trombone or contrabass players, so Leo filled in with his own piano arrangements. Music was still the center of his life, the war merely a far-off dissonance.

But there was room in the foreground for romance. Horenstein was impressed with Leo and urged his sister Augustine, herself an aspiring pianist, to come and hear him. One night, wearing an eye-catching mauve chiffon dress, she did. At the concert's end—so the story goes—she forgot to applaud, stunned by the performance and, perhaps, the performer's looks. Leo was thirty-one, "Gisa" twenty-three. Later, backstage, Horenstein introduced them, and they shook hands warmly. That was how my parents met.

The elegant young woman became my father's student, but the lessons were soon just a pretext for meeting. Leo proposed, but Augustine, it transpired, was already married. It had been an arranged marriage, but her husband was faithful and they had a son; she couldn't desert them, and divorce, in any case, was a scandalous prospect. She saw no future together with Leo. In wartime, however, love can seem more urgent than convention, and the two continued to meet. In 1917 the unfolding drama of the Russian Revolution drew the emigrés even closer together.

As the war dragged on, the upper classes began to lose their wealth and position, and Augustine's family was no exception. Her father, originally from Kiev, was in the sugar beet business, but first he lost his employees to the army and later he lost his farms and refineries to the revolution. Married three times, he had sixteen children. With his third young wife, Marie, he lived quietly in an apartment in Vienna, waiting for the storm to pass. Augustine, however, realized that even after the war her father was unlikely to regain his former prosperity. The days of tutors and governesses (one for every two children) were over. There would no longer be sixteen servants who required their own cook because the family's cook was too busy. No more four-horse carriages (when my grandfather reduced the carriage to one horse, my mother refused to ride in it when they promenaded in the Prater on Sundays). No more trotting through the villages near their estate on the border between Germany and Russia, throwing coins to the peasants (the coins were washed before the children touched them). No more silver beer jugs with hidden mechanisms that played catchy tunes as the beer was poured out. No more dresses from the best couturiers or jewelry from Paris or trips to Karlsbad for "the cure."

It must have been around this time that an incident occurred that forced my mother to formulate her lifelong philosophy about money and its uses. Inflation was already so steep that the money she got from selling a piano one day bought her only a dress and a loaf of bread the next.

"A woman should only have a few things," she told me firmly, years later: "a good fur coat, an elegant suit, a beautiful diamond ring, an evening dress and a good painting. With those she can travel anywhere— at short notice, if necessary."

The war continued into its fourth year. Augustine saw her father and stepmother now and then, and sometimes even gave parties, but the dazzling white tablecloths and the illustrious guest lists were things of the past. The artists who had painted her portrait, the writers who worked her bons mots into their novels, were all at the front. The sound of pianos in the salons was replaced by the clip-clop of hooves and the rattle of carriage wheels as people moved out of the city. Augustine was still in love with Leo, but their world had changed. Music had been forced into the wings.

In November 1918 the fighting finally stopped. The Austro-Hungarian Empire fell, and with it the seven-hundred-year-old Hapsburg dynasty came to an end. A republic was declared. The following January, the Versailles Conference began. Amid all these sweeping political changes, the arts began to revive. Tired of war and eager for cultural sustenance, people started going to concerts again and Leo Sirota suddenly found himself in demand.

After the war, Berlin became a mecca for Russian emigrés, giving a boost to the musical life of the German capital. At the center of it was the conductor Sergei Koussevitsky, who in 1921 invited Sirota to Berlin to perform the Rubinstein and Tchaikovsky concertos. These were a hit. The *Musical Courier* of December 1, 1921, wrote of a soloist "who, with his virtuosity, his passionate temperament and engaging personality, has literally taken Berlin by storm" and went on to predict "a brilliant future for this young man, equipped as he is with all the weapons of the virtuosos of the 'grand' period." The Tchaikovsky, said the reviewer, "had all the variety and color, the melancholy and triumph—the life, in short—that it only has when it is interpreted by a master of Slavic origin... Do the Russians have a monopoly on pianism?"

Sirota's Berlin triumph was repeated in cities across the breadth of Europe and under the batons of the most eminent conductors of the period, including Carl Nielsen and Bruno Walter, not to mention Horenstein, Koussevitsky and Busoni. A critic from the *Wiener Morgenzeitung* in his adopted city of Vienna described him as "one of the last representatives of the disappearing type of great virtuosos, like Liszt and Anton Rubinstein." His conquest of the European musical world seemed almost complete.

It was not proving so easy to win Augustine, however. Leo continued to write to her when he was on tour, and whenever he stayed somewhere for any length of time he received letters from her. But, even in Vienna, he could not always meet her. She was, after all, married and a mother. At this point Busoni, who was an indefatigable arranger, intervened, inviting the two of them to his home for lunch. While Mrs. Busoni engaged Leo in conversation, Ferruccio took the opportunity to advise

Augustine that "Leo is a very nice fellow and an outstanding musician."

Under this sort of pressure, she decided eventually to cut her ties. Leaving her husband to take care of their son, who was just starting to talk, she got a divorce, and in 1920 she and Leo were married.

Before long, the couple's apartment at Waehringerstrasse 58 became a meeting place for artists and intellectuals. Richard Strauss, Kurt Weill, Alma Mahler and Koussevitsky were among those attracted by the conversation, the music and, not least, the Viennese and Russian food, which was beautifully served. My mother's skills blossomed with her guests' appreciation. Not having the support of a famous father, as Cosima Wagner did, she had to depend on her cuisine and conversation to run the kind of salon that would be useful to her husband. Having given up her only son for him, Augustine saw it as her mission to do everything she could to further his career.**

I was born in October 1923. My mother named me after the book *Frau Beate*, by the Vienna-born author Stefan Zweig, whose work she loved. My father liked the sound of "Beate Sirota" and readily agreed to the name.

At that time, Adolf Hitler was already a visible—and audible—presence in Germany. Wearing a *Hakenkreuz* armband, he spoke in the plazas and streets, wherever he could get a hearing among the growing masses of unemployed and disaffected. The Jews, he thundered, were not only responsible for this terrible inflation, they were planning to subjugate the world. Fear battened on ignorance. Without fully understanding Hitler's message, many Germans were ready to participate in his crusade to "save" Germany. My parents, unfortunately, were oblivious to the danger. Absorbed in their baby and their music, the two of them lived as if in a dream.

I don't remember much about my childhood years in Vienna. My mother told me that when my father was practicing, she used to put me in a dresser drawer on top of the piano. The bright sounds filled the whole apartment and seemed to excite me.

According to my mother and aunt, I was a sociable child. Even as a four-year-old, I would ask visitors who came when my parents were out, "Would you like something to eat or drink?" Presumably, I was imitating my mother.

Never shy, I could be relied upon to entertain the guests at her parties.

"Which composer do you like best?" one asked me.

"Stravinsky," I answered promptly.

The guest was wide-eyed.

"Did you hear that?" he said to his neighbor. "She likes avant-garde music."

Even in Vienna, the music capital of the world, not many pianists were playing Stravinsky then. Artur Rubinstein had been engaged to perform in the premiere of the piano version of *Petrushka*, but was unable to prepare it in time, and my father stood in for him. I had heard him practicing this piece for weeks. Stravinsky was probably the only composer's name I knew.

My childish precocity was not always so well received. When I was four, my mother had her portrait painted by a certain Viennese artist. Growing tired of the frequent sittings, she told my nanny she was sorry she had agreed to the project since the painting would probably just turn out to be "kitsch." I asked what that meant. A few weeks later, the portrait was finished and the painter invited us to the unveiling at his studio.

"How do you like it?" he asked me.

"I think it's beautiful," I replied, "but my mama says it's kitsch."

The painter never spoke to my mother again.

Although he lived in another country, my father was very conscious of being Russian, yet he felt he couldn't possibly go back after the revolution. In a sense, he no longer had a homeland. I am not sure when my parents took out Austrian citizenship, but I am certain that the situation in Russia was behind their decision to do so.

After the first evening of my father's return from his year-long tour, the idea of going to live in Japan was not mentioned again—at least, not in my presence. But my parents soon found themselves compelled to leave Vienna anyway. In the aftermath of the First World War, Austria and Germany experienced devastating inflation. There was a sense of instability throughout Europe. Concerts scheduled across the continent had to be canceled. My mother reluctantly came to the conclusion that, provided it was only for six months, perhaps it would be better to go to the Far East. In six months, the Austrian economy might have picked up. With this expectation, we left the apartment in the hands of an agent and, in the summer of 1929, left Vienna. The Wall Street crash took place just two months later, setting off a worldwide depression.

We traveled from Vienna to Moscow and on to Chelyabinsk, where we transferred to the Trans-Siberian Railway. This was my first train journey, and I was thrilled. I soon made friends with the train's conductor, whom I followed around the cars while my parents played poker. In the crew's quarters I distributed the chocolates that had been given to our family by relatives and friends when we left Vienna.

"This is for you," I said grandly, as I handed out the boxes, "and this is for your children at home."

"Are you sure your mother knows about this?" the conductor asked.

So I asked her, and of course she agreed.

The last stop was Vladivostok. Although we were booked into a supposedly good hotel, the bed was already occupied by fleas and bedbugs. I was put up in the home of a musician friend of my father's, while my parents wrapped themselves in the sheets and sat up in armchairs all night. The next day, we boarded the ship for the last stage of the journey across the Japan Sea. Four weeks of travel finally lay behind us as we entered Yokohama harbor. To me, a child from landlocked Vienna, the port was an awe-inspiring sight, with numerous small boats moving about like ants between the towering passenger ships lying at anchor.

The men on the tugboats caught my attention. With their black hair and sallow skin, they looked nothing like the men in Vienna. And then there were the women, with their smooth, porcelain skin, their flat, expressionless faces and narrow black eyes. Both men and women had black hair.

"Mama, are they all brothers and sisters?" I asked.

My parents looked at each other and smiled.

This is my earliest memory of Japan.

My parents had come for six months, but they stayed for sixteen years, and I was there for ten.

* Artur Rubinstein, *My Young Years* (Knopf, 1973).

** The author wishes to thank Joan Kelly Allison for the use of material from her "Remembering Leo Sirota," to be published in the *International Piano Quarterly* in 1998.

Me at nine months, Vienna, 1924.

A birthday party at our house in Nogizaka, 1933 (I am the only child in the room). Mio-san is standing, second from left, between two other maids.

The Sirotas on holiday, 1935.

In Karuizawa, at thirteen, 1937.

Aged fourteen, with a portrait of my father.

With a friend after a performance at the American School, 1938.

3

The House in Nogizaka

I shook my "spoils of war" with both hands. The clicking sound made by the cold marbles I'd just won heightened the feeling of victory, and I clicked them together faster as I went down Nogizaka Hill in Tokyo. The sky was apricot-colored and the woods of Nogi Shrine were growing dark.

Pattering past in their wooden clogs, passersby greeted each other.

"The days are getting short, aren't they?"

"Yes, it gets dark early in autumn, doesn't it?"

Though not quite six years old, I already understood a little of their conversation. It was a peaceful scene in the late afternoon light.

The house where my parents and I had been living since arriving in Japan a few months earlier stood in the third row of dwellings at the bottom of Akasaka's Nogizaka Hill. Four brownish Western-style houses stood next to each other like four friendly sisters. We lived in one of them. The other three were occupied by a singer named Nobuko Hara, a German businessman and a middle-aged White Russian gentleman. The German was a bachelor, but his housekeeper and her family lived with him, and he was helping to pay the children's way through university.

I could hear strains of Mozart, which meant that my mother was teaching. Students who weren't yet ready to study with my father were prepared by my mother.

Hearing the Mozart made me happy. I had an unusual amount of news to report to my mother today. Knocking my marbles together like castanets, I reached the house. Usually I would call "Tadaima!" (I'm home) in a loud voice, but because the piano lesson wasn't over I quietly opened the front door and went straight through the hall into the kitchen.

"Ah, Beate. Welcome home."

Our cook, Mio-san, was busy preparing the evening meal. She was the second servant introduced to us by the painter Ryuzaburo Umehara, who lived at the top of the hill. The first had been a timid, delicate young woman from the village of Enoura in Numazu. Unhappy in a household where hardly any Japanese was spoken and where she was expected to cook only Western food, she had soon gone home. Her successor, Mio-san, also came from Enoura. Umehara used to visit this picturesque coastal village several times a year to sketch, and came to know the place so well that all his servants were from that area. When this eminent but gregarious artist heard that a famous pianist had moved into the neighborhood, he wanted his daughter to take lessons from him. Umehara had studied in Paris with Gauguin, so he and my parents found they had things in common. They were soon on the best of terms. For my mother, helpless and isolated in this new country, the generous, French-speaking painter was a godsend. She asked him about details of everyday life and consulted him about household help, which is how Mio-san came to work in our house.

With the boundless energy of an eighteen-year-old, Mio-san rose to the challenge of serving as my mother's right hand in the kitchen. She was a fisherman's daughter and could clean fish and chop food faster and better than anyone I have ever known. That night, she was mixing oil and vinegar for the salad. She'd been taught by my mother that a dressing had to be mixed quickly and thoroughly.

"What kind of mischief were you up to today, little one?"

Without stopping her work, she turned her face toward me and laughed.

"Do you know what makes this sound?" I asked, using both hands to clink the marbles.

"It must be marbles," she guessed.

"How come you know?" I cried, obviously deflated.

Mio-san laughed. "You know the word 'nanda' (how come)? Little Beate is smarter than her mama and papa. You learned to speak Japanese in three months. That's wonderful. You're a genius. Do you know what 'tensai' (genius) means?"

Mio-san looked at me while her hands continued their busy movements. When I shook my head, she put down the eggbeater, clapped her hands and laughed again.

"The genius doesn't know what a genius is—that's funny!"

Mio-san's laughter made me happy and I laughed too. The kitchen was filled with the sharp smell of the salad dressing. Skipping about with my marbles, I noticed a pail of water in a corner of the kitchen. There was a big carp lying still at the bottom of it.

"It's for tomorrow's party, isn't it?" I said.

"Young lady, you *are* pretty smart," Mio-san nodded. "You have to soak carp overnight so that the mud drains away."

The carp was motionless, as if it knew its fate. When I touched it with a finger, it splashed with its brush-like fins.

"You're with Mio-san again," a voice said from behind me.

It was Miss Kiolein, my governess, who had joined our household to teach me English. A Christian Scientist from Estonia, she had taught the children of an American businessman for several years, but they were now grown up. She had been looking for a new position when she heard that a pianist from Vienna wanted a governess for his daughter.

"You came back just in time," she said in English. "We'll wash your hair before dinner." She repeated the words in German. I was just starting to learn English, but having been born in Vienna my German was fluent.

"I'm looking at the carp," I said in Japanese, in a bid to get Mio-san's support, but I knew it was hopeless. My parents had told me to obey Miss Kiolein unquestioningly. I followed her reluctantly to the bathroom.

"Cover your ears with both hands and close your eyes," Miss Kiolein said. She was still speaking when hot water started pouring over my head. I smelled the English soap, and then the foamy water got into my eyes. Miss Kiolein used both hands to scrub my hair as roughly and vigorously as if she were washing a pair of muddy galoshes. I closed my eyes and started to count. At fifty, then sixty, her hands were still scrubbing. Over and over again the hot water sloshed down.

"It's hot, it's hot!" I protested, unable to stand it any more.

"A little more and we're finished," came the stern reply.

Then I heard my mother's voice.

"Beate says it's hot."

"It's just lukewarm," Miss Kiolein answered, unwilling to back down.

My mother went and fetched a thermometer. "From now on, please use this," she said.

The shampooing was over, but there was another ordeal to be endured: I had to have my hair combed. Since it was curly, it was hard work getting the comb through it. Nevertheless, Miss Kiolein always insisted that her charge be perfectly groomed. When I complained that it hurt, she said, "I comb my hair this way as well," and showed me how she did it. But her chestnut hair was as straight as a Japanese woman's. Instead of arguing, I silently wished I too could have smooth, black hair like Mio-san's.

As soon as my father returned from the Academy, we had dinner. Miss Kiolein ate with us, so we were four at the table. Mio-san and a servant who cleaned the house ate Japanese food in their own rooms. Like many expatriates, we maintained a Western lifestyle, and both the bathtub and the toilet, for example, were Western. Only the servants' quarters were in Japanese style. They had a Japanese toilet but no bath, so Mio-san and the other girl had to go to a nearby bathhouse. Behind the scenes, Mio-san was all-important in our household, but the relationship between employer and employee was a traditional one.

"One of the great virtues of this country is the politeness of its people," Miss Kiolein remarked at dinner. She had been living in Japan for almost ten years and knew much more about the place than we did. A large woman in her thirties, she had the air of someone constantly about to deliver a lecture.

"Another of their virtues is their love of cleanliness," she continued. "They bathe every day."

"That must be why you like Japan," my father said with a smile.

"But it's strange," my mother interjected. "They're such clean people, yet there are so many children with lice and trachoma." This was surprising coming from her, since she didn't get around much.

"It is a result of poverty," Miss Kiolein declared. "Brothers and sisters share a single towel and thus spread diseases. The depression that has been going on in Europe and America is here, too; there are a great number of unemployed in Japan. And the victims of poverty are the children," she concluded, shaking her head.

While my mother cut the cake into neat slices, she told us she'd heard that in northeastern Japan the combination of cold and poverty was forcing people to sell their daughters to brothels.

"The brokers are thugs, apparently, and their numbers are growing," she said. "I also heard that there are municipal agencies, even in Tokyo, for selling women like that."

Despite my age, I wasn't excluded from this discussion. I never forgot it.

At dinnertime the four of us always talked about our daily experiences in this strange land. I showed my parents how to play a Japanese game of marbles on the table, which seemed to quite impress them. And when I told them about having lunch with my Japanese friends and eating six bowls of rice, they laughed. But there was trouble in the offing. In the candy box where I kept the marbles, my mother discovered a ring I'd put away.

"Oh, where did you get this?" she asked.

I said nothing and looked down. She waited expectantly for an answer.

"I got it from Akara Umehara," I said reluctantly.

"But it's a ruby—it's valuable. Tell me how you got it."

I confessed that two days ago I'd been playing with the painter Umehara's eldest daughter. Ten-year-old Akara had proudly showed me her special treasures. Among them was the ruby ring. I was instantly attracted to the stone, which looked like a red currant.

"Please give it to me. Please!" I urged her.

Akara-san, who was always generous to me, said firmly, "No, you can't have it."

That made me want it even more. At this point her mother came over.

"If Beate-san wants it so much, you should give it to her," she said, and she put the ring on my finger.

Akara-san started to cry.

"I'll give you something of mine to replace it," Mrs. Umehara promised, to cheer her daughter up.

The more she heard, the more dismayed my mother was. It seemed that since Mrs. Umehara had gone to all that trouble, it would be insulting to give it back. The result was that I kept the ring for seventeen years. It was only after I returned to Japan when the war was over, and learned that my friend Akara had just had a baby girl, that I was able to hand it back, in celebration of the event.

We had originally expected to stay in Japan for six months, but those months passed quickly. When my parents heard that conditions in Europe were growing worse, not better, and that the Nazi Party had been runner-up in the German elections of 1930, it was an easy decision to postpone our return. Besides, in those six months we had taken root. Kosaku Yamada, our family's sponsor, had lent us his support from the beginning, but we had also been befriended by Hidemaro Konoe, the cofounder with Yamada of the New Symphony Orchestra. It was not long before members of other aristocratic families—the Tokugawas, Mitsuis and Azabukis—started visiting us. Many of them had become fans of my father's after hearing him perform.

To help build a following, my mother resumed her customary party-giving; and just as she had done in Vienna, she quickly earned a reputation as a hostess. Preparations for a party began the day before, with Mio-san working under my mother's strict supervision. The five tradesmen who came every day—the fishmonger, the butcher, the egg seller, the grocer and the beer-and-wine seller—were given their special orders. Mio-san treated them all to tea and crackers, with each one shouting "Much obliged!" as he took off on his bicycle. Since there was no telephone in the house, Mio-san used to send the other servant to Goto's Flower Shop to phone in an order for whiskey to the Roppongi Cocktail Lounge. Using her pidgin Japanese and gestures, my mother managed to communicate her instructions to Mio-san about cooking and serving. "Sara sayonara" (goodbye, plates), for instance, meant "Take the plates away, please." Mio-san, being sharp-witted, understood perfectly. Although she had never seen a table knife and fork in her life before coming to Tokyo, she quickly showed that she could meet my mother's high standards. In no time at all, she learned to make a white sauce so smooth it was like silk on the tongue. She could set dough to rise for the night, and was soon turning out everything from piroshkis to Jewish favorites. Her gefilte fish and tongue were unforgettable. Jewish guests who found these specialties being served so far from home were both amazed and appreciative. Mio-san's repertoire also included minced carp and trout with eggs and onions, made into dumplings and boiled in soup. Since this dish took a lot of time to prepare, even Jews in Europe did not often get a chance to eat it.

All preparations were finished three hours before a party was due to begin. After arranging the flowers and putting out the place-cards, my mother took a bath and a short nap. Mio-san went to the bathhouse, then she too slept for a while. Once the party began, the kitchen became a battleground. Mio-san and a helper or two brought out the food as they had been taught to do, artistically arranged on large platters. The menu consisted of as many as fifteen different dishes. At the end, the dessert was carried in—Viennese Sachertorte or a jelly roll. Everything, of course, was homemade. After the party, Mio-san cleaned up until about 2:00 A.M. and then disappeared till noon, when my mother would report in detail what the guests had said about the food: "The tongue just melted in one's mouth," etc., etc. Within a year, the Sirotas' cuisine was famous in Tokyo.

On one occasion Mio-san's cooking "cured" a celebrated artist's illness. When Fyodor Chaliapin, the Russian *basso*, came to Japan, he caught a cold. My mother heard about this from his manager, so she had Mio-san make some soup with a whole chicken in it and sent her off to his room in the nearby Imperial Hotel. Mio-san changed into her best clothes and, nursing the pot of soup, got into a taxi with a worried look on her face. Two hours later, she returned to the house, her eyes glowing.

"When I told the bellboy I'd come to see Mr. Chaliapin, he looked at me suspiciously," she recounted. "But when I told him I was a servant at the Sirota house and that I'd come to deliver a get-well gift, he finally took me up to his room. Chaliapin-san looks like the polar bear at Ueno Zoo, doesn't he? Such a big man! I was so surprised. When I showed him Madame's letter, he said that he'd already eaten, but would just have a taste of the soup. He took the bowl, had a mouthful, said 'Mmmm...' and then moved the spoon back and forth from the bowl to his mouth without saying a word. I stood there wondering whether I should go home. He kept eating, never saying a word. When the bowl was empty, he smiled for the first time and said, 'That was delicious.' He also ate half of the chicken, smacking his lips. What an appetite the man has!" Mio-san's coal-black eyes twinkled as she told the story.

My mother nodded, satisfied. When they went to see him after his concert the next day, Chaliapin embraced my mother and announced in a booming voice, "This woman saved my life!"

When I turned six, I began taking lessons in "interpretive dance." My mother let me do this on condition that I practice the piano, which she had recently started to teach me. My instructor was an American named Forrest Garnett, who had been a member of Anna Pavlova's ballet company. I loved the dance classes and went to his studio three times a week. I even practiced at home. While my father's pupils took lessons on the floor below, I improvised dances to the music wafting up through the floor. Then, when I got tired of this, I would sneak downstairs to see who was playing. My father charged thirty yen a week for four half-hour lessons, which was as much as the fee for graduate students starting in professional music schools, but this didn't seem to put anyone off. Some of his pupils, not much older than I was, were exceptionally talented. I would see them, brought by their mothers, patiently waiting on the sofa for their turn.

Finding it impossible to compete with these children, I gradually lost my enthusiasm for piano practice. Although I was only a child myself, I had always attended my father's concerts and had heard other first-rate artists, and I already understood the difference between a good performance and a merely adequate one. I also understood my father's attitude toward his most gifted students. He was looking for people who might someday become his artistic heirs. In the tradition he himself had benefited from in Kiev and, later, in Vienna, he felt it was the musician's mission to pass on his knowledge to the next generation. But, musically at least, I knew I could never be his heir.

His youngest pupil was a nine-year-old boy of great intelligence and self-confidence, whose own father was a music teacher. Listening to my father play, the boy was so absorbed he seemed to be hypnotized. But when Leo moved aside to let him play, the boy came to life, playing with remarkable vigor. My father would lean forward and listen intently. Although I couldn't see his face, it was clear to me that he had great hopes for him. His name was Takahiro Sonoda, and indeed later he became a world-class pianist.

Many years afterward, Sonoda described his lessons with my father.

"When I made a mistake, Professor Sirota would say, 'No, listen,' and play it for me. Since I didn't speak any English at the time, I used my eyes and ears to see how the pedaling or the accent should go. Then he'd say, 'Once more, please,' and I'd go through it again. His Beethoven was played with such quiet power I was surprised by the strong physical effect it had on me. With Liszt, though, I could feel the piano shake—I learned the sheer power of Liszt with my body... If things went well in the lesson, your mother used to treat me to some homemade chocolate roll as a reward. I've never been able to forget that cake."

Another talented student, Haruko Fujita, was six years older than me. The daughter of an international lawyer, she had been born in Germany, so we could all talk to her in German. After Haruko had been studying piano for a year, her father fell ill, but she was allowed to continue her lessons without charge. My mother even ordered a sky-blue dress for her first concert; as an ardent patron of the arts, she felt it was our duty to encourage this gentle and gifted girl. Later, Haruko became the first woman student at Tokyo University and a noted constitutional scholar.

Several hundred students studied with my father in Japan over the years, including those from the Imperial Academy. This was an aspect of his career that was important to both my parents. At the same time, he not only maintained a busy concert schedule but traveled on weekends to the Kansai region, southwest of Tokyo, where he gave recitals and taught students from Osaka and Kobe. (In Jun'ichiro Tanizaki's novel *The Makioka Sisters*, mention is made of a Sirota concert.)

My father was a handsome man and frequently found himself surrounded by wealthy female admirers. This could provoke outbursts of jealousy on my mother's part—a woman who had abandoned a son to marry him and then gone halfway around the world to live with him. I can remember one occasion when a marchioness brought a friend to our house to meet him, and as my father was greeting the two ladies, a chair came tumbling down from the second floor.

When she was in a bad mood, my mother would find fault even with Mio-san. The latter was very popular with the tradesmen, and there was always someone in the kitchen chatting with her. Mio-san gave them cakes and tea.

"We won't have any food left for ourselves," my mother once complained when she saw this.

"I haven't touched the household's food," Mio-san assured her. "I use my own money to buy these things for visitors."

"That must be why you've nothing left of your salary at the end of the week," came the sharp reply.

Whenever things got really bad, Mio-san would pack her bags and return to Enoura. But my mother was the one who suffered most from these absences. It was then up to Mrs. Umehara, the painter's wife, to go and bring Mio-san back. Despite these periodic eruptions, though, life was generally peaceful.

The abortive military coup of February 26, 1936, however, brought a new and disturbing element into our lives. Our house in Akasaka was near the barracks of the Third Regiment. On that day, the road was blocked, and military police were posted in front of our house. My parents and Mio-san, and even I, a twelve-year-old, recognized that it was a dangerous situation, but since two policemen stood watch in front of our house and appeared to be protecting us, we felt safe enough. We soon realized, though, that it was our house that was being watched, and a trivial incident revealed that we were in fact under continual surveillance. When we gave dinner parties, it was my job to make place-cards for the guests. I suggested to my mother one day that the cards of people who came often should be kept and used again. Thinking this was a good idea, my mother called Mio-san over.

"Where are the place-cards from the last party?" she asked her.

Mio-san's answer was strange.

"There are no place-cards," she confessed. "The secret police come all the time asking for the names of guests, and I find it hard to remember foreigners' names, so I turn all the cards over to them, which keeps them happy."

What bothered me most growing up in Japan was the German School in Omori, which I entered when I was six. There were only about fifty students—mostly Germans and Austrians, with a sprinkling of German-Japanese—and it was very strictly run. It was not unusual for the teachers to hit the children. Once, in my first year, I made the mistake of writing the letter "Z" backward and had to stay behind and write it out a hundred times.

I took French, German and English classes there, and since Miss Kiolein was also teaching me at home, I made rapid progress. But the atmosphere in the school went from bad to worse. In 1933, Hitler became Chancellor of Germany, and two years later our teachers were replaced by people who were outright Nazi supporters. The pupils were required to say "Heil Hitler!" every morning and to sing the "Horst Wessel Lied," a patriotic song.

At the end of the term that year, I was given a C instead of an A for "deportment." My parents were surprised and went to the school to inquire about this.

"Your daughter was overheard at a birthday party saying that instead of returning the Saar to Germany it would be better for it to be governed by the League of Nations," they were informed. "The mother of the birthday child heard her. Your daughter's a bad influence."

When we got home, my mother told me: "You don't talk about politics in public places."

I knew that I was Jewish. I also knew from my classmates' conversations about the growing oppression of Jews in Germany. But I never imagined that this kind of prejudice would affect me.

Our Nazi geography teacher ridiculed my drawing of a map of the United States because I had punctured the paper and tried to hide the hole with thick lines, making a mess of it.

"Look, everyone, look what a stupid girl we've got here," he said, holding it up to the class.

This was my first experience of public criticism and I was crushed. My parents decided after that incident to transfer me to the American School in Naka-Meguro. I had heard Germans describing the American School as "Sodom and Gomorrah," so I felt I was taking a step down, even being punished.

During my first few days at the new school I suffered from culture shock, but I soon found that I was more comfortable there. The students were of many different nationalities, including Japanese, and were very easygoing. Teachers and students behaved like friends—the place even seemed a little too informal to me, accustomed as I was to the rigors of the German system. You could bring lunch from home or eat the school lunch in the dining room, whichever you preferred. The girls curled their hair, and during recess they took out little mirrors and primped. Some wore ribbons or fancy barrettes, even jewelry. Boys and girls mixed quite freely. There was one girl in the class who was the "queen bee," deciding who should date whom. I had turned thirteen, but as a newcomer I was not accepted into her circle. When dances were held, I didn't have a date. If Miss Kiolein had still been around I could have asked her advice, but she had left for a new position the previous year.

I was a good, hard-working student, but I was rarely asked to dance; the boys only danced with their dates or the dates of their friends. For two hours at school parties I would be a virtual wallflower, and when I went home I lay on my bed and cried. I wouldn't even go down to dinner. My mother was worried, and would come upstairs. I didn't want her to know why I was crying, but after questioning me on the latest of these occasions, she got to the root of the problem.

"The trouble is that you're trying to find a boyfriend in school. You'd do better trying to find one on the outside," she said decisively, patting me on the shoulder.

That very week she found a date for me, a good-looking young Russian who was a friend of one of my father's students. When I went into the auditorium on his arm at the next dance, the girls from my class all lost interest in their own escorts and flirted with mine. The "queen bee" suddenly became much more approachable. From that day on, I belonged.

My mother—so perceptive, so elegant, so sensible—became the ruling authority in my life. Some of the things she said to me then greatly influenced the course I took in life. For example, I had continued to take dancing lessons enthusiastically, and had improved enough to be partnered by my teacher at one performance. Several days afterward, however, my mother made some devastating comments about it.

"You've developed a sense of expression," she said. "You also obviously enjoy it. But what's most important in dance is basic technique, and yours is at too low a level. Only people with outstanding technique can become outstanding dancers. Your talent is obviously for languages." She went on to describe the miserable life that was the lot of the second-rate dancer, performing in provincial halls, sleeping in seedy hotel rooms, barely eking out a living. I was fifteen, and her words made a profound impression on me. I lost all desire to become a professional dancer. The fact that I didn't resist suggests there was some part of me that agreed with her assessment and saw the wisdom of what she said. My father, too, tended to depend on her judgment in many things.

When one road closes, another usually opens. It was true that I had always liked languages. German came naturally; it was my mother tongue. Japanese I learned almost by osmosis. Since I was only five when I arrived in Japan, it was easy to pick up the language. I played with Japanese children, heard Mio-san speak and had the incentive of wanting to be the sole speaker of Japanese in my family. I had heard Russian spoken by my parents since I was a baby, and as I grew older my desire to learn it for myself became all the stronger—my parents spoke Russian when they did not want me to know what they were talking about. They eventually got me a Russian tutor who came to the house once a week. English I learned from friends in the British Embassy and from my governess, and I started French in the German school. I also studied Latin, Italian and Hebrew before the age of fifteen. I didn't like Latin, because one couldn't speak it. Italian I gave up when I studied Spanish in college, since I tended to get the two languages mixed up. I never really had to make an effort to learn new languages, perhaps because I had started so early. A future in the field always seemed attainable and attractive.

When I graduated from the American School I was fifteen and a half. I had hoped to go to the Sorbonne, but it was 1939 and war in Europe was imminent. My parents decided to send me instead to Mills College in Oakland, California, which was physically closer to Japan than most American universities. Trying to get immigration visas in Tokyo, however, presented one serious obstacle: the American embassy required proof from our country of origin that we had no criminal records. We were Austrian citizens, but at that time Austria had been annexed by Germany, and such proof was unobtainable. A testimonial from the Japanese police would do, embassy officials agreed, but the Japanese police said they did not provide such documents for foreigners. In 1936, the Anti-Comintern Pact had been concluded. Under Hitler's influence, hostility toward Jews had risen in Japan, and by 1939 relations between Japan and America were deteriorating.

My parents used all their connections in the effort to obtain the required documents. Koki Hirota, the former foreign minister and later prime minister, lived near us, and he and my father were acquainted. Mail had often gone to the wrong address because of the confusion between the names "Sirota" and "Hirota," so they had come to know each other. At Christmas, when packages for us were mistakenly delivered to Mr. Hirota, he used to joke, "It's too bad I have to give these back; they seem much better than ours."

My parents went to Hirota-san for help. He immediately called the U.S. ambassador, Joseph Grew, to vouch for our characters, and eventually our visas were granted.

In early August 1939, my parents and I set sail for San Francisco on a Japanese freighter. My parents came too, partly because they did not want me to travel alone and also because it seemed an opportune time for them to get immigration visas and begin procedures for acquiring U.S. citizenship.

Just weeks before, on July 17, the American government had given notice of abrogation of the existing trade agreement with Japan. Knowing nothing of this, I blithely sailed toward an unknown life in the United States of America, my new world.

Leo Sirota with music students at the Imperial Academy, 1934.

Guests (including geishas) at a dinner for Chaliapin, the Russian operatic bass, in 1935. (My parents are standing in the background.)

Tokyo, 1936. Back row, far left: Kosaku Yamada, the man who brought my father to Japan. Next row, left of my father: Joseph Rosenstock, the conductor. Just behind my mother (center): Mrs. Netke, a German singer. Seated at far left: Klaus Pringsheim, a conductor who also taught at the Imperial Academy and was Thomas Mann's brother-in-law.

BSG (standing) at an "interpretative dance" class in Tokyo, 1938.

On board the *Nitta Maru*, returning to Japan for a vacation in 1940. The fair-haired brother and sister are Jack and Barbara Curtis (Adachi), who were also at the American School.

At Mills College in 1941, aged seventeen.

4

In Wartime America

"Play the piano every day," my father was saying. "If you skip one day, you'll need three to make it up. Write to us. We'll write often."

He held both my hands as he spoke, and I listened carefully to every word. My mother's face was tear-streaked. It was August 1939, and I was saying goodbye to them on the dock in San Francisco.

My mother recovered enough to give me some last words of advice. "Don't forget, Beate. A girl is like a white towel: once it's been touched, it's no longer clean. Take care of yourself."

I doubt whether I really understood what she meant by this, but I already knew the basic taboos: no intimacy with the opposite sex until marriage; don't hold hands or kiss in public. When, years later, I accused her of having made me prudish, she said, "I gave you this advice when you were fifteen. I didn't know there would be a war and that I wouldn't see you for a long time, and I certainly didn't think you would follow it so literally when you were in your twenties and on your own!"

When their ship set sail, I watched until I could no longer see it. Loneliness flooded me. Why, I thought, had my parents insisted on going back when so many of our friends were leaving Japan and Europe? What made my father cling to his life there? Why had he stayed in Japan in the first place? He had been a rising star in Russia and Europe, Busoni's favorite pupil. I loved Japan because I had grown up there—I thought of it as home—but what about my father?

The fact was that he had found a comfortable life in his adopted country. He could teach and play almost at will, his students were diligent and respectful, there were always partners available for chamber music, bridge and poker. There was none of the constant travel, the series of hotels or the relentless competition that were the pattern of a musician's life in Europe or America. It struck me that my father had deliberately opted for a "normal" life, a life he could enjoy. My mother, on the other hand, yearned for the drawing rooms of Europe every bit as intensely as he savored the simpler pleasures of Japan. But she gave in to him, as she had given up so much else, because she loved him.

As I thought about all this, my own situation was also beginning to sink in: from now on, I was going to have to fend for myself in this huge, unfamiliar country. The sight of San Francisco bathed in sunlight somehow magnified my sense of isolation. I could not have felt less liberated by this separation from my parents. Not quite sixteen, and painfully aware that I could not go home, I boarded the bus to my American college.

Mills College was a forty-five-minute ride from San Francisco, set in a campus bright with greenery and fragrant with the scent of eucalyptus. The dormitories were elegant white buildings—appropriate, I thought, for a women's college. I had been assigned to a private room in the oldest one, Mills Hall, where I found myself, that first night, feeling nervous and distracted. I would have to wear evening dress for my first formal dinner there. Reluctantly, I took a dress out of my trunk. Long and white, with many narrow pleats, the dress had been designed by my mother and was actually quite pretty, but it was now badly wrinkled. Dutifully, I carried my iron down to the laundry room. The problem was that, up until then, the only things I had ever ironed had been dolls' clothes, using a dainty little iron. I had literally never used a real one. My Japanese steel iron was surprisingly heavy and cold, and I stood there holding it, wondering how on earth one went about the task of ironing pleats. I couldn't help thinking of my parents on board the ship, going home without me, and I burst into tears.

"What's happened?" asked a senior who was passing by the laundry room. When I explained, she said briskly, "So that's all it is," and promptly showed me how to do it.

"I'll do the whole dress for you if you'll lend me your iron for the rest of the semester," she offered. "I don't have one."

My first lesson in America: "give and take" was the way to go.

The next morning brought another problem. I had never made a bed before. Our servants had always done it, just as they had always quietly picked up the clothes I'd thrown on the floor as I got ready for bed. Having grown up with daily household help, I was beginning to think the standard of living in America was lower than in Japan.

Five hundred girls were enrolled at Mills. The president, Aurelia Henry Reinhardt, was a tall, heavy-set widow of about fifty, who was known for her progressive views.

"The women of the future will participate in society, not only in the home," she used to say. "It's important to get married, but if you can have a career and run a household as well, that would be ideal."

Mrs. Reinhardt's suggestion that middle- and upper-middle-class women should work was a novel one at the time, but in accordance with her ideas the Mills faculty all taught as if it were a generally accepted fact that their students would get jobs after graduating. Because I was interested in pursuing a career involving languages, I majored in languages and literature. My French was advanced enough by then for them to have to put me in a special class in French literature, with just one sophomore and one graduate student for company. In my Russian class I was the only student. The biggest class I had was in Spanish, where there were fourteen girls. In Japanese, as in Russian, I was one-on-one with the instructor. This course should have been a joy, but it proved just the opposite. The man must have felt uncomfortable teaching Japanese to a student who was fluent in the language and knew the country better than he did. By coincidence, he was Austrian, and he taught Japanese history in a dull, pedantic manner. Never having been to Japan, he couldn't speak the language, but he could read it to some extent. I was bored. When he expounded his narrow, patronizing views on Japanese family life and urban culture, I had to choke back my objections.

Very few Americans had been to Japan at that time, and knowledge of the country was virtually nonexistent. At parties with students from other universities, whenever I said I was from Japan I was pestered with questions.

"Do they have trains in Japan?"

"Do they live in caves?"

"Do the Japanese really have to wear that funny topknot?"

"Have you ever seen someone commit harakiri?"

Hearing questions as ignorant as these coming even from Stanford University students, I wasn't merely shocked, I was insulted. I took their ignorance personally. When one lives long enough in a country, one begins to identify with it, and I considered myself partly Japanese. The flower arrangements in the tokonoma with the sunlight filtering through the sliding papered doors, the fragrance of the straw matting, the summer festivals when the young men in *happi* coats carry portable shrines through the streets, the cool sound of the wind chimes, the call of the tofu seller, the voice of the itinerant storyteller, the sharp smell of rice crackers … I tried to describe these things, but never felt I got through. I began to pretend I had come to Mills from somewhere in the Midwest.

Collegiate America was a world of parties. Any occasion served as an excuse. One evening I decided to wear a Chinese satin evening gown, a purple thing embroidered with white flowers that fitted me like a sheath, but when I put it on, my next-door neighbor looked askance.

"It looks like a bathrobe," she said bluntly. "In America we don't wear things like that."

I was taken aback. In fact I was so offended I decided to wear the dress to the party anyway. When my date and I arrived at the ballroom at

Stanford, the dress drew admiring comments.

"My, that's beautiful."

"Where did you have it made?"

"Who designed it?"

And even, "May I dance with you?"

Another useful lesson learned in my early days in America: don't let yourself be misled by other people's advice.

Still missing my parents, I gradually began to settle into the college routine. There were ups and downs, of course, the most obvious of the ups being an unexpected weight gain. Eleven extra pounds in three months made my face as round as a marshmallow, and when I put on my beloved Chinese dress, bulges were visible. The culprit was the milk shakes I had discovered in the off-campus coffee shop. These foamy concoctions, which neither my mother nor Mio-san had ever heard of, tasted to me like nectar. I drank one every day and never got tired of them. But before I went back to Japan I decided to diet, and that was the end of the milk shakes.

Summer vacation came early. In May 1940, after final exams, I went home on the liner *Nitta Maru*. The first thing I did in Tokyo was to visit the dentist, having been unable to face the idea of an American dentist poking his large fingers into my mouth. Then I accompanied my parents to Karuizawa, where we spent the rest of the vacation in our summer house. On June 14, 1940, we heard that the German army had entered Paris. In July, it was announced that Japan's Yonai Cabinet had resigned en masse. The sale of luxury items was abolished, but things like imported butter were still available, and outwardly our lives carried on pretty much as before. Even during the summer vacation there were students who came for piano lessons, so I saw familiar faces. With the sliding doors open, I could watch the neighbors' children chasing dragonflies. I read extensively. Happy to be back with my parents, I tried to ignore the slogans that were blazoned all over Japan: "One hundred million with one heart!" "Japan, march southward!" and the like. The days passed quickly.

All too soon I was back in college, resuming my Japanese studies with the same uninspiring teacher. According to him, China and Japan were culturally indistinguishable. Before entering Mills, I had been to Peking and Shanghai, and so knew a little bit about China. My parents had wanted me to see Japan from the outside, as a part of Asia. China and everything in it had seemed overwhelmingly large: the Forbidden City and the Temple of Heaven in Peking, the boulevards, the sheer number of people. Compared to Japan, China had struck me as infinitely more powerful and dynamic—and physically messy, with people spitting and blowing their noses without handkerchiefs, and men urinating in the streets. Shanghai was a city of mixed light and shadow: the French and British quarters bright and lively, but those where the Chinese lived run-down. One couldn't help noticing the effects of aggressive colonization by the West and by Japan.

It was obvious that much of Japanese culture originated in China, but I knew and admired Japan as a country that had also enjoyed two thousand years of indigenous development. Japan may have borrowed its written characters from China, for example, but the two languages are not at all alike today: Chinese word order is very much like that of English, with the verb coming early in the sentence, while in Japanese the verb comes at the very end. My Mills professor, however, did not consider such distinctions important. Nor did he appreciate the Japanese genius for making something out of nothing. Using just three flowers in a flower arrangement, creating a "ceremony" for something as simple as drinking tea, the Japanese have made an art of miniaturizing. But how can you explain the taste of a particular food to someone who has never tried it? I gave up on him. I stayed in his class, but I poured my energy into French instead.

I was active in the campus French Club. When I was a sophomore, I became head of the club and organized occasional parties. Taking a cue from the can-can danced at the Moulin Rouge in Paris, I wanted to use a cabaret theme for one party, but my very proper French faculty adviser thought this would be inappropriate when France was in the middle of a war. So I decided on an "Empire" theme instead. I had club members drape the windows with sheets folded like curtains and taught them to dance the minuet. I was in my element. Years later, when I became director of the performing arts program at the Japan Society and afterward at The Asia Society, it occurred to me that this memorable party may have marked the beginning of my career as a producer.

An important date on my calendar was a visit by my parents, planned for July 1941. I counted the days till they arrived.

When the day finally came, I went to meet their ship, the *Tatsuta Maru*. It was anchored outside the port. There was a U.S. boycott of silk at the time, and since the *Tatsuta Maru* was carrying a cargo of silk, it was not permitted to dock. I had not realized that relations between Japan and the U.S. had deteriorated that far, and I was shocked and agitated.

The next day, the *Tatsuta Maru* was still forbidden to dock. I was afraid the ship would simply turn around and go back. The fact that my parents were Austrian citizens made no difference with the immigration officials; nobody could disembark. This was how things remained for three days. I learned afterward that there had been panic on board when the ship was refused entry, and my father had played the piano to help keep the passengers' spirits up. On the fourth day, permission to land was finally granted, and the three of us had a joyful reunion.

We went to Hollywood, because we knew people there who had fled from the Nazis. Erich Korngold, also from Vienna, who was composing film scores, found us a place to stay in the actress Eva Le Gallienne's apartment. We heard about the triumphs and trials experienced by the European emigrés in Hollywood. But the main thing on people's minds was the likelihood of war between Japan and America.

"Don't worry," my father said, "it won't happen." Through his friend Hidemaro Konoe, the conductor and brother of the prime minister, he was personally acquainted with a number of high-level government officials, and from them he had not got the impression that war was imminent. My mother, however, was sick with worry.

"Let's stay in America," she urged him. "Especially since Beate is here."

My father answered firmly, "I have a contract with the Imperial Academy of Music. I must return to the school. My students are waiting for me."

In September, their ship left San Francisco for Japan, stopping in Honolulu en route. My mother's anxiety was only heightened when U.S. officials in Honolulu told them they could not go back to Japan without FBI clearance. Until permission came through, they had to rent an apartment in Honolulu, with my father giving local concerts to cover their living expenses.

Why, in the face of my mother's and friends' warnings, did my father persist? The answer is complex. He had a strong sense of responsibility and sincerely felt he could not break his contract with the music school. In his ten years in Japan, he had also made a name for himself: he had a large public following. He liked the climate, and he appreciated the relative absence of anti-Semitism. He was also by nature optimistic.

In November 1941, when my parents finally got clearance, they took passage on what turned out to be the last ship from America to Japan. Friends and journalists who went to see them off told me how sad and ominous this particular parting seemed. My parents reached Yokohama at the end of the month.

Ten days later, Japanese bombers attacked Pearl Harbor.

I had gone out with friends that December day. When I returned to the dormitory around 4:00 P.M., there were students talking excitedly in the hall.

"Did you hear?" they called out. "Japan has bombed Pearl Harbor, and there's been a lot of damage. It's war!"

My body turned to stone, though my thoughts raced. At least my parents were no longer in Hawaii—that was a relief. Then I felt a surge of anger. How could Japan be so stupid as to provoke a war with such a vastly superior power? I had no idea what I should do. There would be no more money coming from Japan each month, no more letters. Before he left in September my father had deposited some money for me in a bank, and I knew I could continue to live on that for about six months. My head was spinning. On top of Pearl Harbor, news was circulating of Nazi roundups of Jews in Europe. Dark foreboding was becoming reality.

My studies went on as before, but now we had a new duty—to knit sweaters and mufflers for the troops. Since I was not very good at it, my mufflers invariably had holes in them. While I was knitting I thought of the Japanese girls who were undoubtedly doing the same thing, many of them with fathers and brothers and lovers in mind. I thought of my party-loving mother not giving any parties now, and of my father's concerts, which he must have cut down or stopped altogether. Were the students still coming for lessons?

In Japan, I would learn later, the government had already issued orders controlling foreign mail, requiring very clear writing of the sender's name and address and censoring of the contents. American and English films were forbidden, and jazz was declared to be "enemy music." Even the microphone was considered a subversive device.

I also learned after the war of the particular interest the secret police took in my parents. In 1941, when they sailed on the *Tatsuta Maru* to San Francisco, the Czechoslovakian chargé d'affaires had asked my father to mail some letters for him when he arrived in America. These were in a sealed envelope. Since the man was a pupil of his and a good friend, my father didn't think anything of it. On his arrival in San Francisco, he opened the envelope and found two letters, one addressed to President Eduard Beneš and one to the diplomat Jan Masaryk. He sent them off. When my parents returned to Yokohama in November, the police threatened to arrest my father on the charge of espionage, confronting him with evidence that they knew about the letters he had smuggled out. Fortunately, the father of one of his students was an international lawyer, and when called to the dockside he was able to persuade them that Leo was merely an innocent "postman" and in no way involved in spying. Only then was he released.

As the war continued, my bank balance dwindled. By the summer of

1942 I had no choice but to become self-supporting. I found part-time summer work easily enough at the CBS Listening Post in San Francisco, where I took a job translating radio broadcasts from Japan for thirty dollars a week. Since that was higher than the average wage, I was more than satisfied. But there was a problem: before I could be hired on a more permanent basis, I had to pass a test. When I saw the passage in Japanese I was required to translate, I quailed—it was studded with technical expressions, almost none of which I understood. And, sure enough, to the dismay of someone who had actually lived in Japan for ten years, I failed.

I didn't give up, however. The senior person there suggested I come in every day and listen to the broadcasts to familiarize myself with military terminology; he thought it might just be a matter of getting used to the noisy static of the shortwave broadcasts. I knew it wasn't noise, though, that was the problem so much as my lack of vocabulary and ignorance of the kind of sentence structure typically used in broadcasting. So I set to work. I made a list of military terms used in the San Francisco newspapers and tried to get hold of an English-Japanese dictionary. It seemed there was no such thing to be had in that city. With help from a Russian emigré friend, who came up with a Russian-Chinese-Japanese dictionary, I managed to get my list of English words translated into Russian, then found the Japanese equivalents. After two weeks of study and listening in to Tokyo Radio six hours a day, my efforts paid off. I was monitoring a shortwave broadcast from Japan for practice when suddenly I heard an item about a Japanese submarine approaching San Francisco harbor. My boss, Christopher Rand, happened to be looking over my shoulder and noticed what I'd written. He asked me to make a word-for-word translation from the dictaphone machine we used to record broadcasts. The listening post in Portland, Oregon, which also monitored Tokyo Radio and was staffed by relocated Japanese-Americans, had not picked up this item. I won Rand's confidence on the spot and was hired without further ado.

Just as I was getting used to the work, though, summer vacation ended. My boss asked me to stay on, and I was tempted: the job was interesting and I needed the money; but I also wanted to finish college. Mr. Rand called Mills to plead my case, and it was decided that, as a special concession, I could skip classes and fulfill the graduation requirements just by writing term papers and taking exams. "You have a serious responsibility. Do your best for our country," the college president said, shaking my hand. Although I felt no animosity toward the Japanese in general, I did want to help defeat their military. I also had to support myself, and this job seemed the best means of doing so. At the same time, I was waiting to get U.S. citizenship, for which I had applied many months before.

In September 1942, the CBS Listening Post became part of the FCC (Federal Communications Commission), but though the name changed, the personnel did not. Surprisingly, I was the only woman working there. My daily routine was as regimented as army life: after breakfast, I would immerse myself for several hours in research and writing my college papers, then work from 3:00 to 11:00 P.M., as the JiJi News broadcasts from Japan were heard in San Francisco during the afternoon and evening. We had been assigned to the sixteenth and seventeenth floors of the old Empire Hotel, which was the tallest available building; the antenna was up on the roof. The trouble was, the building was located in the city's most disreputable neighborhood. As night fell, its streets came to life with soldiers and sailors heading for the bars and clubs. By the time I went downstairs at eleven the excitement was at its peak. I was forced to walk along the curb to avoid being pinned against the walls of the buildings by drunken sailors carousing with their girls. It was always a relief to get safely to the cable car at the corner and ride home.

Before long, my salary almost doubled, going up to $50 a week. The apartment I shared with two other girls cost me just $65 a month in rent. Even after deducting food expenses, there was money left over, and I was able to save close to half my salary. Earning and saving my own money was a new and heady experience. As a direct consequence of the war, I found myself largely self-reliant by the age of nineteen.

My work at the FCC also gave me access to information about my parents, as I had hoped it would. My office received daily reports of German broadcasts from our Washington bureau, and one day there was news about an interview given in Tokyo by a pupil of my father's named Sonoko Tanaka.

"You're a student of Professor Sirota's, aren't you?" the interviewer asked.

"Yes. His daughter is in America, but Professor and Mrs. Sirota are here in Japan."

"What is their daughter doing in the U.S.?"

"She's in college in California."

"Did you ever want to study abroad yourself, to take advantage of the musical opportunities available there?"

The transcript of the report broke off at that point, but at least I knew now that my parents were still alive. I also took comfort from the fact that the interviewer should even ask such a question as the last one, suggesting that the atmosphere in Tokyo might not be as repressive as I had feared.

Some time later, however, when my section had a different boss, another message arrived from Washington. The new man, not knowing my background, came to my desk and said, "There's a news item here containing the same name as yours. Do you think it might be a relative?"

I leaped up from my seat. It could only be about my father.

"Kreuzer and Sirota, two Jewish musicians," I read, were being relieved of their duties at the Imperial Academy. They were also barred from playing with any Japanese musicians. How could they do that to my father, who loved Japan and was devoted to his students? Overwhelmed with fear for his safety, I put my head down on my desk and wept. The new director, in an effort to help, suggested I try communicating with him through the International Red Cross, so I ran out and sent a prepaid-reply telegram to Japan, which cost me the huge sum of twenty-five dollars. But I never got an answer.

Day by day, the tempo of the war picked up. In the autumn of that year, 1942, we heard about the naval engagements in the South Pacific, and in January 1943 Churchill and Roosevelt concluded a treaty at Casablanca spelling out the details of an offensive strategy. In February, the Japanese started to withdraw from Guadalcanal, and the Germans surrendered at Stalingrad.

I waited every day for the sound of the name Sirota in a broadcast, but all I ever heard were military reports starting out portentously with "The Imperial Navy…" and degenerating into terrible static. To distract myself, I did nothing all day but work. Although I remembered my father urging me to keep playing the piano, I had neither the time nor the inclination for it. For six months, I went nowhere on weekends and practically gave up going to concerts, movies and dances. My life passed in a monastic round of academic study and FCC translating.

My term paper for the uninspiring professor of Japanese consisted of an extensive Japanese/English glossary of economic and military terms. I had picked up these contemporary terms from the shortwave radio and thought they might be useful somehow in the war effort. The glossary included the Japanese word in both its romanized form and in Chinese characters, along with the English translation.

The professor returned the term paper to me marked D because it had no foreword and because I had listed two or three words in both the economic and military sections. He also pointed out that I had repeated a page number. The dean of the college called me in and suggested that I do the paper again to try to get a better grade. I was reluctant, because it would mean writing out all the Chinese characters again to keep them in sequence on the page, which would take ages. But the dean told me I had been nominated for Phi Beta Kappa and unless I eliminated this D, I wouldn't be eligible. I finally agreed, laboriously redid the paper, and won a grudging B+ for it. I had my revenge later, when I snubbed the man in question at the Phi Beta Kappa ceremony.

Those last six months of college were probably the most grueling of my life. I promised myself I would simply enjoy myself once I got my degree, and so I did; if my old calendars are accurate, I went out almost every night for the next two years.

After graduation, I transferred from the FCC to the Office of War Information. The OWI was also based in San Francisco, but had more regular hours, from 9:00 A.M. to 5:00 P.M. The salary was the same, but the new hours were a welcome change. My job was to produce broadcasts targeted at the Japanese and designed to simultaneously inform and demoralize—San Francisco's answer to the broadcasts of Tokyo Rose, the voice of Japanese propaganda for front-line U.S. troops. The short broadcasts I produced consisted of three minutes of music accompanied by a seven-minute message. I selected the music and wrote the scripts, which were then sent to Portland, where a Japanese-American read them over the air. The reason I did not read them myself was fear of what might happen to my parents if my voice were recognized in Japan intoning "This is the Voice of America. You have been deceived by your military…"

I knew that the Japanese liked being culturally up-to-date, so I used to include modern music they could no longer hear at home, especially Stravinsky. My father's favorite Russian composers were aired, too, on the off chance that he would be listening. The control I had been given over the content of these programs made it a dream job for me.

I wrote hundreds of shows, and yet in Japan after the war I never met a single person who had heard them. Since soldiers' lives were strictly controlled and shortwave radios rarely available, I suppose our broadcasts were listened to by government officials and no one else.

It had once seemed as if the war would go on forever, but by now news of Japan's weakening military position was reaching us daily. There was a group of Koreans working in the broadcast/translation section of the OWI, and whenever they heard reports of yet another Japanese withdrawal, they were jubilant. I remember how complicated my own feelings seemed in contrast to theirs, anxious as I was about my parents' welfare.

On November 3, 1944, I received a small brown package from England. When I opened it, I saw it was an announcement that my cousin Igor had been killed in the Normandy Invasion. I had never met Igor, who was my father's eldest brother's son. The fact that the official notification had come to me in America meant that he had no other known relatives in devastated Europe. I wondered whether they had all ended up in Auschwitz. Thinking about Igor and my other unknown relatives and their fates in Europe, I wanted desperately to make contact with a blood relative. My mother's sister Dascha was a hat designer in New York City, a place I also wanted very much to see, so when one of my roommates decided to try her luck there, it wasn't long before I followed her.

I arrived in New York in March 1945 after a four-day train journey and moved in with my trailblazing roommate. Following an emotional meeting with Aunt Dascha, I then set about job-hunting in a serious way. There weren't many professional positions open to women then, but on the strength of my knowledge of languages and my FCC and OWI experience, I found work in the Foreign News Department of *Time* magazine, doing research for the staff writers covering Japan.

Time's researchers had two tasks: one was to gather material, the other to make sure there were no factual errors in the finished article. Above every word we placed a small dot confirming its accuracy, one of the anomalies at *Time* being that for any mistake printed in the magazine the researcher was held responsible, not the writer. All the writers were men, all the researchers were women. Most of these women, who came from all over the world, had unusual and interesting backgrounds; as far as I could see, they were intellectually far superior to their male colleagues. Yet, in journalism, America's much-vaunted freedom did not extend to permitting women the freedom to write the news. I was not the only one who was indignant about this, but the risk of losing a job that wasn't easy to get was enough to keep us quiet. One day, however, my dissatisfaction erupted. The writer I was working for asked me for material on samurai swords. There were not many books that mentioned the subject in English, but I tracked down a few in the Columbia University Library and the New York Public Library. I also found some Japanese-language sources, which I translated and gave to the writer.

"The samurai sword is double-edged," this man wrote, incorrectly.

"Japanese swords are single-edged, not double-edged," I told him.

"In the book you borrowed for me, it says they're double-edged," he said, showing me one of the English-language sources.

"Then the author made a mistake. In this Japanese book it says there are no double-edged samurai swords."

"Well, I can't read Japanese."

"I lived there for ten years, and I saw the swords with my own eyes," I insisted.

He ignored me. A woman with firsthand experience was evidently not as reliable a source as a man who had had his opinions published.

From the windows of the *Time* offices we could look out toward the Empire State Building. On most days it was just another skyscraper, but when I was angry it assumed a more sinister cast, looming up like a steel embodiment of the masculine power that still excluded women and children from society's ruling structures. This endless war seemed just another instance of where male aggression led. In my agitation, I missed my mother badly. How would she have dealt with people like this, I wondered.

"Stick to your guns, Beate. Fight back," I imagined her urging.

World conditions changed sharply in April 1945; in that month Mussolini was assassinated and Hitler committed suicide. "Invincible" Germany had been defeated. I was readier than ever to leave *Time*; with victory near, the prospect of personal freedom was finally within range.

Early in May, when I heard that the Russian Army had occupied Berlin, I cheered. In my mind's eye, I saw the hated faces of the Nazi teachers at the German School in Omori. Now all we were waiting for was the end of the war in the Pacific. But despite news that Okinawa had been occupied and the fighting in Luzon had ended, the conflict dragged on. And the absence of any word from my parents left me uncertain about their fate.

Their fate, as it turned out, had been that of all "neutrals" in Japan (even though Austria had been annexed by Japan's ally); they were ordered to evacuate to Karuizawa. If aliens were left scattered all over the country, it was thought, they might pick up information useful to the enemy. Better to keep them in one place. The Sirotas closed their house in Nogizaka and had two precious pianos moved to the summer house in Karuizawa. My father had been doing a lot of traveling and thought that a temporary stay in Karuizawa wouldn't be so bad, and my mother, under his influence, took it fairly calmly herself. "At least we have the pianos," they told themselves. How uncomfortable could it be? They had no idea that in winter the temperature there would drop below freezing

There was a shortage of meat in 1942, but life was bearable. By 1943, all the embassies of the Allied and neutral powers not already in Karuizawa moved there. The Russian embassy and the Spanish and Portuguese legations were housed in the fashionable Mampei Hotel, which ultimately served as home to some three hundred diplomats. Karuizawa became the diplomatic center of Japan and a particular focus of interest for the secret and special police. My parents had daily visits from the secret police.

Karuizawa was a summer resort rather than a year-round agricultural area, and getting food became more and more difficult as the war went on. To begin with, most of the basic necessities were available at the Swiss legation, which occupied the Mikasa Hotel. The Swiss had arranged with the Japanese government for special rations to be allocated to the European community, including meat, sugar, fish, wine and milk, but not clothing. There were stamps for bread, which could be bought at the bakery. But supplies of all kinds dried up as the military situation got worse. The remarkable thing was that even during the direst shortages, there were no reports of violence. And people discovered unsuspected funds of resourcefulness in themselves. One Frenchman kept a goat and a beehive. My mother searched in the woods for mushrooms and found some she thought were similar to those used in Russian cooking; she learned that if she used a silver spoon while cooking them, she could tell the poisonous ones from the good ones, as the poisonous mushrooms would blacken the spoon. She dug a hole in the ground to store sweet potatoes in so they would not freeze. She kept a chicken whose own survival instincts were, apparently, quite strong. One day, it flew up into a tree and could not or would not get back down. My mother tried to help it down with a stick, but she couldn't reach up far enough. The chicken refused to budge. At that moment, the secret police arrived for the daily interview.

"Anything new here?" they asked as usual. "Have you received any letters?"

"Don't keep asking me the same questions all the time!" my mother snapped. "For once, why don't you do something useful? Like getting that bird down from the tree for me."

Seeing her standing there clutching her stick and glaring, one of them took a long pole and chased the hen off its branch.

The secret police watched every aspect of my parents' lives. The fact that I was living in enemy territory was obviously cause for grave suspicion, which wasn't helped by their being on such friendly terms with the diplomats in Karuizawa. As Japan's military reverses mounted, the fear that these foreigners might be receiving reports by shortwave radio and signaling to the enemy in the dead of night increased.

My father was forbidden to teach any Japanese pupils. He continued to play at least three hours a day, but since he could not work he had no income, obliging my mother to begin giving piano lessons to the women and children of the Swiss and Spanish legations in exchange for food. The local people were afraid to sell food to foreigners, thinking the secret police might target them as well if they did so.

One day my father took a cashmere sweater to the house of a farmer who lived nearby to barter with. He stood in the entranceway for a long time, but no one appeared. He knew the farmer was not allowed to sell him anything, but he kept going back. Finally, one day, when he opened the door, the farmer stuck his head out.

"Where have I seen you before?" he asked. "Are you the one I saw, or are you somebody else?" He cocked his head, looking my father up and down, and withdrew. After a few moments he reappeared. "It *is* you," he said, smiling, and led him into the living room. On the wall hung a poster advertising a concert my father had given in Tokyo. From then on, the farmer secretly gave him whatever food he could.

Food was not the only thing needed to survive in Karuizawa, however. By October, you needed firewood. Although my mother was unhappy about letting him do it, my father used to go into the forest to gather wood so regularly that it became his principal occupation. "In war, pianists do not play—they gather wood," became one of my mother's sayings.

In 1944, conditions grew even worse. The number of people sequestered in Karuizawa grew. Eight hundred of them came from the island of Hachijoji, where gun emplacements and a signal corps base were being built. All the men of the island had been recruited by the army, and the old people, women and children were moved to the mainland. Those who did not have relatives or friends they could stay with were brought to Karuizawa. The people of Hachijoji were not used to the cold, and many fell ill. Then the evacuation of schoolchildren from Tokyo began. The Karuizawa Elementary School took in four hundred and eighty transfer students in the first wave; by 1945, nineteen hundred children were enrolled.

On July 31, 1945, my parents had their biggest scare. The secret police came as usual, but they told my father to report in a week's time to the police station, where he would be held for questioning. My parents were terrified, and endured a week of sleepless nights.

On August 6, the atomic bomb was dropped on Hiroshima. The news spread quickly. That was the day my father was supposed to present himself for questioning, but, of course, he did not go. Nothing happened. Nor did the secret police come the next day.

At the news of Japan's surrender on August 15, New York erupted. Complete strangers hugged and congratulated each other in the streets. I was as thrilled as any of them, but simultaneously I was consumed with worry about Tokyo. Reports were that it had been devastated by air raids. What had happened to Mio-san and her children, to the Umeharas, to

Haruko Fujita? Had the gifted Sonoda's piano been burned to ashes? And then there were my elderly parents, of whom I'd heard nothing all these years. I had asked a *Time* correspondent who was going to Japan to try to find out what had happened to them, but the weeks of waiting passed very slowly.

The telex from John Walker finally arrived on October 24. "Tell Miss Sirota her parents are well and okay. They apparently got out of Tokyo before the big fire raids and have been living since in Karuizawa..." This news marked the real end of the war for me. All that day I was walking on air, and in the evening my roommate and I drank champagne.

I started looking for work that would take me to Japan. On my days off, I went to Washington and ferreted out whatever information I could. The Foreign Economic Administration, I heard, was looking for people to participate in organizing the Occupation under MacArthur. I applied without further ado. Since I spoke Japanese and had already worked for the FCC and OWI, I was hired almost as quickly. That was the end of my stint at *Time*. On Christmas Eve, 1945, after a five-year absence, I came home.

My father's passport. Note the large "J" (for "Jude") stamped on it.

BERLIN (TRANS)CEAN) IN ENGLISH AT 9:00 AM TO NORTH AMERICA

(TEXT) "TOKYO—THE JAPANESE MUSICAL CULTURE ASSOCIATION PASSED
A RESOLUTION FORBIDDING ITS MEMBERS TO PLAY TOGETHER WITH ARTISTS
OF COUNTRIES WHICH DO NOT BELONG TO THE AXIS. AMONG ARTISTS WORKING IN
JAPAN ARE SEVERAL JEWS WHO HAVE LOST THEIR GERMAN CITIZENSHIP.

"KREUZER AND SIROTA, TWO JEWISH MUSICIANS, ARE ENGAGED AS
TEACHERS AT THE MUSIC HIGH SCHOOL OF TOKYO. THEIR CONTRACTS
EXPIRE NEXT JUNE. TWO OTHER JEWISH MUSIC TEACHERS, GURLITT AND PRING-
SHEIM, STILL HAVE THEIR GERMAN NATIONALITY AND THEREFORE DO NOT
COME UNDER THIS NEW DECREE ACCORDING TO THE ,TOKYO SHIMBUN,."

AMC 12/14-9:40A

The message announcing my father's dismissal from the Imperial Academy.

My official ID card.

Generals MacArthur and Whitney leaving GHQ Tokyo.

A *Time* magazine cable sent in October 1945: "Tell Miss Sirota her parents are well and okay."

Col. Charles Kades and myself revisiting Mac-Arthur's office in Tokyo, 1993.

During the Occupation, 1946.

Civil Rights Comm
Wildes, Roest
Sirota

GENERAL HEADQUARTERS
SUPREME COMMANDER FOR THE ALLIED POWERS
Government Section
Public Administration Division

MEMORANDUM FOR THE CHIEF, GOVERNMENT SECTION.

The Committee on Civil Rights submits the following report:

CHAPTER III

CIVIL RIGHTS

I. GENERAL

Article I   The people of Japan are entitled to the enjoyment without interference of all fundamental human rights [that
do not conflict with the equal enjoyment of those rights by
others.] deleted by 2/12/46

Article II   The fundamental human rights hereinafter by
this constitution conferred upon and guaranteed to the people of
Japan result from the age-old struggle of man to be free. They
have survived the exacting test for durability in the crucible
of time and experience and are conferred upon this and future
generations in sacred trust, to be held for all time inviolate.

Article III   The freedoms, rights and opportunities provided
by this Constitution are maintained by the [self-disciplined
cooperation] of the people. They therefore involve a correspond-
ing obligation on the part of the people to prevent their abuse
and to employ them always for the common welfare.

Article III (joining art I   The feudal system of Japan shall cease. All
Japanese by virtue of their humanity shall be respected as in-
dividuals. [Their right to life liberty and the pursuit of happi-
ness (within the limits of the general welfare) shall be the
supreme consideration of all law, and of all governmental action.]

BSG (waving a white handkerchief) leaving Japan in 1947.

◀ A page of the second draft of the new constitution.

Lt. Joseph Gordon, at twenty-six.

Wedding day: Jan. 15, 1948.

The Equal Rights Clause

February 4, 1946, was a cold Monday in Tokyo. A harsh wind blew, and week-old snow lay in grimy patches among the ruins.

Here and there wisps of smoke rose from the air-raid shelters that many families were using as homes. Most of those whose houses had burned down in the raids had gone to stay with relatives outside the city, but these people obviously had no one to take them in. After more than a month in the city, I was still saddened by the sight of meager breakfasts being cooked in the mornings and hungry children wrapped in futons poking their heads out of the shelters. And these were the lucky ones. Some families had no breakfast at all.

As usual, I left my billet at the Kanda Kaikan at 7:30 and walked to the Dai-Ichi Insurance Building opposite the Imperial Palace moat. At 7:55, when I arrived, I sensed something different in the air in the former ball-room that served as our office on the sixth floor. My cheerful "Good morning!" met with silence. It was soon apparent that the "upper crust" of the Government Section, Col. Kades and his top assistants, who often arrived a little late, were already hard at work.

Puzzled, I went to my desk and started working too. The first phase of the political purge, which had been announced on January 4, was being administered by the Government Section, and I was well into my assigned task of researching minor political parties and women in politics. At ten o'clock, the twenty-five members of the Government Section (everyone except the group overseeing not-yet-independent Korea) were summarily ordered to assemble in the adjacent conference room. It was not a very large room, there were not enough chairs, and about half of us had to stand. Ruth Ellerman, the oldest of the six women on the staff, was ready with her notebook in her hand.

Gen. Whitney appeared, confirmed that everyone was present, then addressed us.

"Ladies and gentlemen," he said. "Today you have been called here as a constituent assembly. General MacArthur has given us orders to do the historic work of drafting a new constitution for the Japanese people."

The atmosphere was electric.

Whitney, then forty-nine years old, was MacArthur's closest adviser and had taken over as head of Government Section on December 15, ten days before I was assigned there. He now produced a memo and proceeded to read it aloud. This memo, later dubbed "the MacArthur Note," contained three principles:

> I. The Emperor is the head of state. His succession is dynastic. His duties and powers will be exercised in accordance with the Constitution and responsible to the basic will of the people as provided therein.

> II. War as a sovereign right of the nation is abolished. Japan renounces it as an instrumentality for settling its disputes and even for preserving its own security. It relies upon the higher ideals which are now stirring the world for its defense and its protection. No Japanese Army, Navy or Air Force will ever be authorized and no rights of belligerency will ever be conferred upon any Japanese force.

III. The feudal system of Japan will cease. No rights of peerage except those of the Imperial family will extend beyond the lives of those now existent. No patent of nobility will from this time forth embody within itself any National or Civic power of Government.

"This draft," Whitney continued, "must be finished by February 12, when we're required to submit it for General MacArthur's approval. On that date the foreign minister and other Japanese officials are to have an off-the-record meeting about the new constitution. We expect that the version produced by the Japanese government will have a strong right-wing bias. However, if they hope to protect the Emperor and to maintain political power, they have no choice but to accept a constitution with a progressive approach, namely, the fruits of our current efforts.

"I expect we'll manage to persuade them. But if it looks as though it might prove impossible, General MacArthur has already authorized both the threat of force and the actual use of force.

"Our objective is to get the Japanese to change their ideas on constitutional revision. They must agree to accept this kind of liberal constitution. They must, in short, cooperate with our aims. The complete text will be presented to General MacArthur by the Japanese for his endorsement. General MacArthur will then announce to the world that he recognizes this constitution as the work of the Japanese government."

I knew nothing about the Japanese constitutional drafts at that time, but it was clear from talk around the Government Section that the kinds of reforms that had already been proposed to the Japanese government by the Occupation authorities had triggered sharp dissension.

"We will suspend our regular activities," Whitney concluded. "And remember, what you write during this coming week is to remain top secret."

He headed back to his office, leaving the staff buzzing. Already mindful of the injunction to secrecy, however, we buzzed quietly. Col. Kades now took charge, explaining how the work would be broken down and who would be assigned to what.

Kades himself was to run the Steering Committee, which would include Lieutenant Colonel Milo E. Rowell, a constitutional expert, and Commander Alfred R. Hussey, head of the Legislative Division. Seven other people were assigned to chair the other committees, one of which, the Civil Rights Committee, was to be headed by Col. Roest. Dr. Wildes and I were listed as members. I felt a little shiver of pride at that moment as I thought of my parents' hopes for me.

Of course, one week was far too little time in which to write a new constitution, but the feelings of excitement and idealism that everyone seemed to share swept all such worries aside. There would always be time for repairs; hadn't the U.S. Constitution itself undergone countless revisions? Still, it was an enormous undertaking. I listened in silence to the scholarly discussions that immediately broke out on civil rights and the limitations to the Emperor's powers. At the age of just twenty-two, I was in awe of all these specialists; what little I knew of such matters came straight from my high school social studies classes. Despite or perhaps because of this, I felt a tremendous sense of mission and was determined to do my best. I was also encouraged by the feeling that both Col. Roest and Dr. Wildes trusted me.

The practical business of producing a draft required each committee to divide up the work that fell to it. The matter was sometimes decided quite summarily.

"You're a woman; why don't you write the women's rights section?" Col. Roest said to me.

I was delighted.

"I'd also like to write about academic freedom," I said boldly.

"That's fine," Roest smiled. I had been given a plum, and here I was already demanding another. But I welcomed the responsibility, feeling all the more committed.

What kind of provisions would be necessary to secure the rights of Japanese women? It struck me at once that the best approach to the problem would be to read other constitutions. My research experience at *Time* stood me in good stead here. I got Roest's permission to leave the building and quickly requisitioned a jeep and driver from the motor pool so I could visit various libraries in Tokyo. Within a few hours, I had collected a dozen or so books containing the texts of a whole range of constitutions, including those of the Weimar Republic, France, the Scandinavian countries and the Soviet Union, as well as the U.S. Constitution and the Declaration of Independence. I was amazed that these books were still available in a city that had been so thoroughly bombed, especially since some of them were in English. When I returned to the office, my arms full, the whole Government Section flocked around me.

"These are great sources," people said.

"Can I borrow this for a while?"

My sudden popularity acted like a shot of adrenaline. I read all afternoon, along with everybody else in the section. As we sat there silently turning pages, we could have been students cramming for a particularly important exam.

A scanty lunch was served on the seventh floor, but by evening I wanted a proper dinner, so I put away my books, documents and memos in the safe and left for the Kanda Kaikan. As I made my way down the narrow aisles between desks, other staff members were still immersed in their work.

In February, it is dark in Tokyo by 6:30. I walked briskly, a cold wind on my face, but I didn't get back in time for the seven o'clock dinner hour. That night my head was full of thoughts about drafts and constitutions, and I slept fitfully. Being hungry certainly did not help.

Tuesday, February 5

At eight o'clock the next morning when I entered the office in the Dai-Ichi Building, the stale smell of cigarettes hung in the air. All morning long, I plowed through constitutions and made notes. The Weimar and Soviet documents were the most intriguing. The Soviet Constitution, for example, had been enacted in 1918, on the heels of the revolution, and spelled out specific rights for women. The U.S. Constitution I had studied at the American School, but rereading it now I saw that civil rights were not protected by the original document of 1789, but only later, in amendments. Women's suffrage, for example, was not guaranteed until 1920, with the passage of the 19th Amendment.

While I read, I tried to imagine the kinds of changes that would most benefit Japanese women, who had almost always married men chosen for them by their parents, walked behind their husbands, and carried their babies on their backs. Husbands divorced wives just because they could not have children. Women had no property rights. It was clear that their rights in general would have to be set forth explicitly. I went through my notes and underlined the points I believed it would be essential to spell out: equality in regard to property rights, inheritance, education and employment; suffrage; public assistance for expectant and nursing mothers as needed (whether married or not); free hospital care; and marriage with a man of her choice.

Washington had provided guidelines in the form of broad statements of principle, which could be construed as authorizing such things, but neither the MacArthur Note nor the old Imperial Constitution mentioned civil rights even in passing. It would be our job to introduce the concept to Japan in a detailed and concrete way.

Formulating a text proved to be a complicated business. Linguistic pitfalls abounded. It turned out, for example, that language frequently used to provide legitimate exceptions in civil rights guarantees—"except as provided by law"—had been used wholesale in Japan in the past to violate civil rights. It was daunting to think we had only a week to get it right.

By the afternoon, Underwood typewriters were clacking all over the former ballroom. As soon as I decided to make "Men and women are equal as human beings" the key words, I turned to my typewriter as well. As I saw it, my mandate was to ensure that civil rights and equal opportunities would be articulated in as practical and specific a manner as possible. The most important unit in human relations, it seemed to me, was the family, and within the family the most important element was the equality of men and women.

"The family is the basis of human society," I began, "and its traditions for good or ill permeate the nation. Hence marriage and the family are protected by law, and it is hereby ordained that they shall rest upon the undisputed legal and social equality of both sexes, upon mutual consent instead of parental coercion, and upon cooperation instead of male domination. Laws contrary to these principles shall be abolished, and replaced by others viewing choice of spouse, property rights, inheritance, choice of domicile, divorce and other matters pertaining to marriage and the family from the standpoint of individual dignity and the essential equality of the sexes."

I went over my typed article many times, trying to ensure that I had covered the rights of wives adequately and in such a way that there could be no legal misinterpretation. I even consulted the relevant Japanese Civil Code. Although I spoke Japanese fluently, my reading and writing were far from perfect, but, using a dictionary and commentaries, I read the old code carefully. "Women are to be regarded as incompetent," stated Article 4. They could not sue, they could not own property; they were, in effect, powerless. Naturally, they did not have suffrage.

On October 11, 1945, Gen. MacArthur had decreed, among other things, the emancipation of women and their right to vote. A look at the past reveals what a revolutionary change this was for Japanese women.

Women do not feature prominently in Japanese history. They started off auspiciously: Amaterasu, a goddess endowed with supreme authority, is the first deity recorded. A handful of empresses have graced the imperial line, and the Heian period (794–1192) was a kind of literary golden age for women, its most notable figure being Murasaki Shikibu, author of *The Tale of Genji*. But even then their social position was entirely subservient to and dependent on that of men. Later, when the samurai established the shogunate, it declined even further. Women were little better than chattel to be bought and sold.

Col. Kades thought it might be a good idea to refer to the Meiji Constitution of 1889 in writing the draft, but to me it was useful only in emphasizing the need for change. It accorded the Japanese people the status of subjects of the Emperor, with very limited privileges. The provisions for religious freedom were conditional, for instance, and there was no mention of national responsibility for health and welfare. If the Emperor's male subjects were so little regarded, one can imagine how lowly the position occupied by women was.

In the end, the model for my draft text on women's rights was the 1919 Weimar Constitution, a progressive document that saw marriage as based on the equal rights of both sexes. It was the duty of the state to promote social welfare policies supportive of families, and motherhood was guaranteed government support. As a woman, I felt that my participation in the drafting of the new Japanese Constitution would be meaningless if I could not get women's equality articulated and guaranteed with similar precision.

I don't know how many times I revised my draft. I kept changing the wording, inserting phrases in pencil and typing it again. Every time I reread it, new ideas came to me. When I finally looked up, I saw that it was dark outside. Cigarette smoke swirled up toward the high ceiling. I got up and opened a window. The night air touched my face, and I could see the shadowy bulk of the Imperial Palace looming opposite.

My watch read six o'clock. If I didn't get back to the Kanda Kaikan in time, I would miss dinner again. Feeling that I had accomplished something genuinely important, I decided it would be all right to stop, even though the others were all still at their desks and Col. Kades was still writing.

Wednesday, February 6

Someone brought in a newspaper dated February 5, which carried a small article about the Japanese government's efforts to write a new constitution. Working since January, it reported, Home Minister Matsumoto had prepared an article-by-article explanation of drafts A and B of a proposed revision. A Cabinet meeting that day was to discuss it. There was no hint in the piece that GHQ was in any way involved in these matters; the Government Section had apparently been successful in keeping its work "top secret." I had not even phoned my parents recently, knowing I would be unable to answer questions about what I was doing at work.

After reviewing the draft I had written the day before, I turned to the specific issue of the rights of mothers. "Expectant and nursing mothers," I wrote, "shall have the protection of the State, and such public assistance as they may need, whether married or not. Illegitimate children shall not suffer legal prejudice but shall be granted the same rights and opportunities for their physical, intellectual and social development as legitimate children."

It was my understanding that if I wrote specific women's rights into the constitution, legislators would not be able to disregard them when devising the new Civil Code. I knew that the vast majority of the bureaucrats likely to be responsible for wording the provisions of the new code would be men, and conservative men at that, especially in their attitudes toward women.

The Japanese women who had attended my mother's parties in the old days had often talked about mistresses and adopted children. I remembered one of them saying, with raised eyebrows, "Mistress and wife live side by side in that house."

"What a terrible thing," my mother had replied.

They talked angrily of men who, without bothering to ask their wives, brought home and then adopted children they had fathered outside marriage.

"If it were me, I might even have agreed to it, if I'd at least been consulted," one woman said.

I wrote: "No child shall be adopted into any family without the explicit consent of both husband and wife if both are alive, nor shall an adopted child receive preferred treatment to the disadvantage of other members of the family. The rights of primogeniture are hereby abolished."

Poorer children were often deprived of an education. Among our neighbors in Nogizaka was a German bachelor who had his Japanese housekeeper and her children living with him. One of her sons was a particularly good student, and the German paid his tuition all the way through college. Remembering this boy now, I wondered what would have happened to him without our neighbor's support.

I continued: "Every child shall be given equal opportunity for individual development, regardless of the conditions of its birth. To that end free, universal and compulsory education shall be provided through public elementary schools, lasting eight years. Secondary and higher education shall be provided free for all qualified students who desire it. School supplies shall be free. State aid may be given to deserving students who need it."

I remembered the friends I had played with in Nogizaka, tossing lumps of coal about in the street on cold winter days. As the scene came back to me, I saw again the boy with the runny nose, one of his eyes inflamed by trachoma, and the girl with a cheek swollen by toothache and wrapped in a towel, gamely playing hopscotch.

"The children of the nation, whether in public or private schools, shall be granted free medical, dental and optical aid," I wrote, drawing on an article in the Soviet Constitution. "They shall be given proper rest and recreation, and physical exercise suitable to their development."

Through my mother and our housekeeper, Mio-san, I was aware that, before the war, farmers had been known to give away their children in order to cut down on the number of mouths to feed. Such children were forced to leave school and earn their keep; their only pay was a kimono every six months. During famines, girls were sold off. Col. Roest used to mention this at meetings. There should be a place in the constitution for children's rights, too, I thought.

"There shall be no full-time employment of children and young people of school age for wage-earning purposes, and they shall be protected from exploitation in any form. The standards set by the International Labor Office and the United Nations Organization shall be observed as minimum requirements in Japan."

That evening I made it in time for dinner at the Kanda Kaikan, and then returned to work. Other people, too busy to leave, were eating sandwiches in the seventh-floor cafeteria. Everybody was working late. Our typist, Edna Ferguson, and I finally returned to our billet at ten o'clock, but most of the others stayed on.

Thursday, February 7

A fierce wind was blowing from the west, out of Mongolia. Feeling impatient, I went to the office earlier than usual. The others must have been similarly affected, since almost everyone was there. Some of the staff had worked through the night. Both Roest and Wildes were red-eyed.

I had completed a draft of the section on women's rights, as well as the clause on academic freedom, in the space of two days. I sat down and read what I'd typed, edited it, typed it again, and waited to show it to my colleagues. While waiting, I looked through the various constitutions again to see if I had missed anything. Believing that this was a chance Japan would never have again, I wanted to be sure not to omit a single thing that might benefit Japanese women in the future.

Roest and Wildes labored on at their desks, beyond distraction. As they finished each page, they handed it to Miss Ferguson to be typed. Dr. Wildes had been a journalist, a professor and an editor, and thought himself a stylist; unfortunately, he was forever adding words and phrases to pages that had already been done, imposing quite a burden on the typist. I felt sorry for her.

By the end of the day, our committee had not yet finished its draft, since Roest and Wildes were still adding to the text. Our deadline was February 8—tomorrow. Roest, who as committee chairman bore the responsibility, showed signs of tension and fatigue.

Friday, February 8

The early morning sky was overcast, with snow predicted before nightfall. The meeting with the Steering Committee was set for today, which meant there was a good chance I would be going home late, in the snow. I took a big scarf with me. After four days without enough sleep I felt exhausted. I thought I would wait for a jeep to pick me up in front of

Kanda Kaikan, but I was afraid that it would be full and I wouldn't get a ride. I saw streetcars going by packed with people. I thought of taking one, but rejected the idea, since I knew they were off-limits to Occupation personnel. So I set off again on foot.

The big front doors of the Government Section office were closed. Using a side entrance, I found Roest and Wildes still correcting their drafts, showing signs of having worked all night. Off to one side, Miss Ferguson was already typing.

There were to be three copies of the draft for the Steering Committee, double-spaced to allow for changes. Since there was no such thing as a Xerox machine in 1946, we made carbon copies. Mistakes had to be erased on all copies, so we always had carbon-stained fingers. Finally, by mid-morning, our drafts were ready.

The Steering Committee room was full of cigarette smoke from the previous meeting when we entered. The committee members, Kades, Rowell and Hussey, were waiting for us, along with Commander Guy Swope, an expert on administration. Ruth Ellerman stood by, notebook ready. As he presented our voluminous forty-one-item draft, Col. Roest sighed and said, "There's quite a lot of it, I'm afraid." We felt a twinge of foreboding, which turned out to be warranted.

There were disagreements from the outset. The Steering Committee rejected an article that reserved general unspecified rights for the people. They took out an article forbidding members of the clergy from entering politics and another one restricting the grounds for dismissal of teachers. They also objected to an article that stated, "No future constitution, law or ordinance shall limit or cancel the rights guaranteed in this constitution." By the time it was my turn to discuss the various articles I had drafted, it was one o'clock.

The three-man committee read my text in silence, while I sat with the palms of my hands beginning to get damp. The reaction came quickly and quietly.

"Your basic point, that says 'marriage and the family are protected by law, and it is hereby ordained that they shall rest upon the undisputed legal and social equality of both sexes,' is good, but in general the draft should be more concise."

I was encouraged, but a sigh of relief was premature. The committee went on to dissect, minutely and critically, each of the articles I had contributed to the draft.

Articles 19 to 25, concerning social welfare, embodied my heartfelt wish that women and underprivileged children in Japan should benefit from such important rights as free education and medical care. Col. Kades raised his eyes from the draft and looked at me.

"Concrete measures of this sort may be valid," he said, "but they're too detailed to put into a constitution. Just write down the principles. The details should be written in the statutes. This type of thing is not constitutional material."

I argued that the bureaucrats who would be assigned to write those statutes for the Civil Code would undoubtedly be so conservative they could not be relied on to extend adequate rights to women. The only safeguard was to specify these rights in the constitution. But it was no use: the committee continued to insist on wholesale cuts. Feeling outnumbered, I nevertheless tried again.

"Colonel Kades, social guarantees are common in the constitutions of many European countries. I believe it's particularly important to include this sort of stipulation here because up to now they had no such thing as civil rights."

Roest lent me his support. "It's true," he said, "—legally women and children are the equivalent of chattel in today's Japan. At a father's whim, preference may be given to an illegitimate child over a legitimate child. When the rice crop's bad, some farmers actually sell off their daughters."

"But even if we do put in rights for expectant and nursing mothers and adopted children," Swope objected, "conditions won't improve unless the Diet enacts the laws that will implement them."

To this, Wildes replied: "That's true. But we can make certain that the Japanese government is committed to doing that. It's absolutely necessary. Infringement of civil rights is an everyday affair in Japan. There's a word for 'people's rights' in Japanese, but 'civil rights' doesn't exist."

Before I could add anything to this, Rowell cut in.

"It isn't the Government Section's job to establish a perfect system of guarantees," he said categorically. "If we push hard for things like this, we could well encounter strong opposition. In fact, I think there's a danger the Japanese government might reject our draft entirely."

Flushed and agitated, Dr. Wildes resumed the argument.

"We have the responsibility to effect a social revolution in Japan, and the most expedient way of doing that is to force through a reversal of social patterns by means of the constitution."

In answer to this seemingly unanswerable claim, Rowell said:

"You cannot impose a new mode of social thought on a country by law."

Even though it was apparent to everyone that GHQ was changing many of the old ways of Japan, we had no effective counterargument to this. Much of what I wanted to say remained unspoken. It was like being in court, but a military, not a civil, court, and the Steering Committee ultimately had the upper hand.

They started to cut out the women's social welfare rights one by one. With each cut I felt they were adding to the misery of Japanese women. Such was my distress, in fact, I finally burst into tears. That Col. Kades, whom I respected so much, should fail to accept my point of view was a major disappointment. While I wept he patted me on the back, but he remained adamant in his rejection of my proposed text.

The discussion went on late into the night, but we didn't even get halfway through our draft. The basic disagreement on social policy was so serious that the Steering Committee felt they should take it up with Gen. Whitney. His decision was to leave out detailed policies and to include instead a general statement providing for social welfare protection. This confirmed Kades's view. The upshot was that my articles 17 and 18, as listed below, were left more or less intact, though shortened, but all the others (19 through 25) were eliminated.

III. Specific Rights and Opportunities

17. Freedom of academic teaching, study, and lawful research are guaranteed to all adults. Any teacher who misuses his academic freedom and authority shall be subject to discipline or dismissal only upon the recommendation of the national professional organization to which he belongs or in which he has a right to membership.

18. The family is the basis of human society and its traditions for good or evil permeate the nation. Hence marriage and the family are protected by law, and it is hereby ordained that they shall rest upon the undisputed legal and social equality of both sexes, upon mutual consent instead of parental coercion, and upon cooperation instead of male domination. Laws contrary to these principles shall be abolished, and replaced by others viewing choice of spouse, property rights, inheritance, choice of domicile, divorce and other matters pertaining to marriage and the family from the standpoint of individual dignity and the essential equality of the sexes.*

19. Expectant and nursing mothers shall have the protection of the State, and such public assistance as they may need, whether married or not. Illegitimate children shall not suffer legal prejudice but shall be granted the same rights and opportunities for their physical, intellectual and social development as legitimate children.

20. No child shall be adopted into any family without the explicit consent of both husband and wife if both are alive, nor shall any adopted child receive preferred treatment to the disadvantage of other members of the family. The rights of primogeniture are hereby abolished.

21. Every child shall be given equal opportunity for individual development, regardless of the conditions of its birth. To that end free, universal and compulsory education shall be provided through public elementary schools, lasting eight years. Secondary and high-

er education shall be provided free for all qualified students who desire it. School supplies shall be free. State aid may be given to deserving students who need it.

22. Private educational institutions may operate insofar as their standards for curricula, equipment, and the scientific training of their teachers do not fall below those of the public institutions as determined by the State.

23. All schools, public or private, shall consistently stress the principles of democracy, freedom, equality, justice and social obligation; they shall emphasize the paramount importance of peaceful progress, and always insist upon the observance of truth and scientific knowledge and research in the content of their teaching.

24. The children of the nation, whether in public or private schools, shall be granted free medical, dental and optical aid. They shall be given proper rest and recreation, and physical exercise suitable to their development.

25. There shall be no full-time employment of children and young people of school age for wage-earning purposes, and they shall be protected from exploitation in any form. The standards set by the International Labor Office and the United Nations Organization shall be observed as minimum requirements in Japan.

I do not remember when we finished the discussion that day, I only remember the coffee we drank and the cigarette smoke. I don't even remember eating dinner. When I went back to my desk in the ballroom, everybody was still working, their eyes now chronically bloodshot.

I headed home. The wide road was blanketed with snow, as had been forecast. From inside the hooded jeep I stared at the swirling flakes. I was still too upset to repair my makeup, ruined by tears. To this day, I believe that the Americans responsible for the final version of the draft of the new constitution inflicted a great loss on Japanese women.

Saturday, February 9

The weather that weekend was very cold, with unusual amounts of snow for February. The grounds around the Diet, which had come through the bombing unscathed, looked like a winter scene painted by an old master. To add to the general misery of the Japanese, bad news seemed to be coming as thick and fast as the snow that now lay heaped up around the city. The newspapers that week had reported the suffering of women and children living in schools that had survived the raids. Prices had gone up four hundred percent. The black market was thriving. General Yamashita, the former commander in the Philippines, had been sentenced to death. There was also the news that various Pacific islands, including Okinawa and Saipan, were to become trust territories of the United States.

It was warm enough in the Government Section when I went in. The Steering Committee had not had time to go over all forty-one articles of our draft on Friday, so the session was extended one day. I did not attend this part of the meeting, however, since I was working on corrections and changes to my own segment.

Roest and Wildes tried again to get as many of the social guarantees as possible into the constitution, but they were generally unsuccessful. It was interesting to see two men of such wide differences in background and personality finding themselves in such deep agreement on the matter of our draft. In view of that, I was surprised to read later, in his book *Typhoon in Tokyo,* that Dr. Wildes considered Col. Roest a man of little ability.

If it had been an ordinary Saturday, we would have worked until three o'clock, but the meeting ended much later. It was decided that the completed draft of the constitution would be given to MacArthur the next day, Sunday the tenth.

At that stage, the Civil Rights Committee had been left with thirty-three of its original forty-one articles, roughly one-third of the total number of articles in the proposed constitution.

On the way home late that night, the roads gleamed with ice. The week that had begun on February 4 seemed in retrospect like a single, seamless piece. It felt as if we had been working not for six days, but for weeks.

The question arises as to why MacArthur was in such a hurry to have the constitution drafted. One reason could be that the Far Eastern Commission, made up of eleven former Allied powers, was due to be established on February 28. Since this body included countries such as the Soviet Union, Australia, New Zealand and China, which opposed the imperial system that MacArthur intended to maintain, it was important to get the Japanese government's approval of the constitution as soon as possible. In addition, a general election had been scheduled for April 10, the first since the war; it would be important to have the voters give their judgment on the new constitution, so as to conform to the Potsdam Declaration's stipulation, "... in accordance with the freely expressed will of the Japanese people."

Because of the time it would take to make and transcribe revisions, the Civil Rights Committee was given until February 12 to work on a final draft. Forty-one articles had shrunk to thirty-one by the final stage. From my specific point of view, we had at least succeeded in including a statement guaranteeing in principle the rights of women and children. In this important area, the new constitution completely superseded the Meiji document.

On the night of February 12, the full ninety-two-article draft was completed. All that day, Gen. Whitney, the members of the Steering Committee and the heads of all the other committees had met in a last effort to perfect the document. The debate between the pragmatists and the idealists continued, with the former prevailing in their preference for a streamlined draft, but the latter very much dictating its underlying spirit. In the end, benevolence rather than vengeance emerged as the dominant principle guiding the efforts of everyone who helped frame the constitution.

The finished draft ran to twenty pages, double-spaced. Thirty copies were made and signed by the compilers and presented to MacArthur. I and two others did not sign, because we weren't present when Col. Kades called for signatures. It was very late, so late that the twenty-five of us who had worked so hard for the past week were too tired to celebrate. After nine days, the lights on the sixth floor of the Dai-Ichi Building were finally switched off, and everybody went back to their billets.

On February 13, the draft was given to Foreign Minister Yoshida and Home Minister Joji Matsumoto at the foreign minister's official residence. The American delegation, consisting of Gen. Whitney and the Steering Committee, told the Japanese officials that the draft submitted earlier by the Japanese government was completely unacceptable. In view of the Japanese draft's failure to broach the issues of freedom and democracy, SCAP was proposing that its own draft be taken as the required basis for the new constitution. The SCAP officials then withdrew to give the other side time to analyze the document.

The Japanese officials were shocked. They had expected to discuss the Matsumoto draft with the Americans, not to be presented with an entirely different document. After they read it, they were even more shocked. When Gen. Whitney came in again to respond to their questions and objections, he pointed out that MacArthur himself was under great pressure from various quarters to treat the Emperor as a war criminal and that a new constitution, complete with all the required guarantees, could well assist him in resisting such pressure. To the Japanese, this was tantamount to a threat. The formulas guaranteeing democracy and equality, which to us were the chief end of all our efforts, were not things they could easily accept.

This first meeting lasted only an hour and ten minutes. The Japanese presented a copy of the SCAP draft to Prime Minister Shidehara, and then Matsumoto prepared yet another version, which contained no reference whatever to civil liberties. This was also rejected, as was a subsequent draft. On March 4, in a joint session designed to bring the two sides together face to face, another revised draft was presented by the Japanese. That morning, Col. Kades called me.

"We can use as many interpreters as we can get," he said. "Please come to the meeting."

I was glad of the chance to see in person what happened to the civil rights articles I had written.

The meeting took place at 10:00 A.M. on the sixth floor of the Dai-Ichi Building. Because of SCAP's determination that this constitution be viewed as Japanese in origin, the proceedings were designated top secret, and we were told we could not leave the building until they were over.

The Japanese contingent consisted of Home Minister Matsumoto, Tatsuo Sato, the head of the First Department of the Legislative Bureau, Jiro Shirasu, deputy chief of the Central Liaison Office, and Kunryo Obata and Motokichi Hasegawa from the Foreign Office.

The Government Section, represented by Gen. Whitney and Kades, Rowell and Hussey, sat with the Japanese around a large table. The team of translators was headed by Lieutenant Joseph Gordon, a capable and quick-witted intelligence/language officer. I was the only woman in the room.

Matsumoto started by handing his draft to Whitney, being careful to explain that this was not a formal version approved by the Cabinet. The Japanese would be using this draft as a basis for negotiation. Col. Kades immediately turned his copy of the document over to the language team. As each article was translated, he studied it closely.

The opposing viewpoints of the two parties were clear from the outset. The very first article of our draft, for example, contained a reference to "the sovereignty of the people." The Japanese had revised it so as to remove these words. This, Kades insisted heatedly, was unacceptable. The Japanese revision appeared to be designed to preserve the exalted position of the Emperor. There were lengthy arguments about the true meanings of words preferred by the Japanese, which seemed to the Government Section to represent attempts to water down the American text. My throat became dry as I and the other translators explained the significance of numerous disputed terms. The discussions were generally polite, but tense; nobody wanted to concede anything. The Japanese side continued to maintain that the terms demanded by the Government Section were not "proper" for a constitution, and the Americans continued to disagree.

By 2:30 virtually no progress had been made. Since we were not permitted to leave the conference room, we ate lunch at the table. We were provided with C and K army rations (C came in cans and K in boxes), both barely adequate. The discussions became more heated, until Matsumoto, fearing that there might be no room for compromise, turned authority over to Sato and left to report to the Cabinet on the gravity of the situation.

That evening, Lt. Gordon noticed a literal Japanese translation of the Government Section's English draft lying unremarked on the table near him, apparently left there by the man from the Central Liaison Office. Once Gordon realized what he was looking at, he knew that the draft put forward by the Japanese had become irrelevant. This was their way of signaling that they had given up a losing battle. They had come to the meeting prepared to surrender, but had used it to make a last-ditch effort to promote their own version. From that point on, the task of translating became easier. Discussions continued, but the rancor had eased.

It was not until 2:00 A.M. that the civil rights section came under consideration. Everyone was tired. Nevertheless, to my great surprise, the Japanese started to argue against the article guaranteeing women's rights as fiercely as they had argued earlier on behalf of the Emperor. This article, they felt, was "inappropriate" for the Japanese. Although I had been fighting sleep, I snapped awake when I heard these arguments.

The Japanese had taken a liking to me, probably because I was a fast interpreter. Col. Kades, ever sensitive to nuances in people's feelings, thought to take advantage of this to forestall further argument.

"This article was written by Miss Sirota," he announced. "She was brought up in Japan, knows the country well, and appreciates the point of view and feelings of Japanese women. There is no way in which the article can be faulted. She has her heart set on this issue. Why don't we just pass it?"

There was a stunned silence from the Japanese, who had known me only as an interpreter. But to my delight the ploy succeeded.

"All right," they said, "we'll do it your way."

The remaining articles were not accepted so readily. The so-called "Red Articles," which gave ultimate ownership of land and natural resources to the state, met with such strong opposition that they were dropped. The unicameral system of government proposed by the Government Section was changed to bicameral. With ninety-two articles to consider, we still had a long way to go at 3:00 A.M.

Negotiations continued into a wintry dawn. More C and K rations. Soon it was ten o'clock. The air in the room was stale, and the people around the table had dark rings under their bloodshot eyes. I was finally told I could leave. When I reached my billet I fell into bed and slept like the dead.

After I left, discussions over terminology resumed. The step-by-step process seemed interminable to those who stayed, but it finally ended at 6:00 P.M. on March 5, thirty-two hours after it had begun. GHQ wanted to announce the completion of the draft immediately, but the Japanese government preferred to wait until the next day, citing the time it would take to present the new constitution to the Cabinet, the Emperor and the Privy Council.

On the evening of March 6, the revised draft was published as the work of the Japanese government. Gen. MacArthur announced that he was fully satisfied with the "new and epoch-making" constitution, as if he had never seen it in his life.

But it was the banner headlines in the next day's newspapers that reflected the common reaction best: "New Constitution Draft Rejects War." Only the article renouncing militarism really touched the hearts of people who had suffered such devastating losses.

From then on, my work no longer involved the constitution, and there was much to occupy me outside the office. My father needed a new environment in which to resume his music, and my parents had decided to move to America. Before I knew it, their departure date, May 22, was upon us. Haneda Airport was just a flat meadow then, but to my father it was the beginning of the road to New York and the rebirth of his career.

I was lonely in Tokyo without my parents, but the work in the Government Section was still interesting and I had another reason, too, for being in no hurry to return to America. I had begun to see Lt. Gordon socially. He was handsome in his dark khaki officer's uniform and had a dry sense of humor. We enjoyed each other's company. After eating one frugal and indigestible lunch with me at my billet, he kept leaving food on my desk and asking me out to dinner at the elegant officers' club and to movies at the Ernie Pyle Theater.

On November 3, 1946, the Japanese Constitution was promulgated. When the Emperor read the imperial rescript, his hands seemed to tremble. Unnoticed, the members of the Government Section who were still in Tokyo sat together in the House of Peers. Six months later, on May 3 of the following year, the constitution went into effect. After its promulgation, Prime Minister Yoshida sent a silver saké cup to everyone who had taken part in drawing it up, and I received some white imperial silk as well, from which I had blouses made. The silver cups given to the twenty-five people in the Government Section were engraved with the imperial chrysanthemum emblem. Why was that, I wondered, when the occasion was the passage of a democratic constitution? It seemed inappropriate.

My silver cup is on a shelf in our house. Together with the cup given to my husband, Lt. Gordon, we have a matching pair.

---

*This became Article 24 of the promulgated constitution, which reads:

> Marriage shall be based only on the mutual consent of both sexes and it shall be maintained through mutual cooperation with the equal rights of husband and wife as a basis.
>
> With regard to choice of spouse, property rights, inheritance, choice of domicile, divorce and other matters pertaining to marriage and the family, laws shall be enacted from the standpoint of individual dignity and the essential equality of the sexes.

With Fusae Ichikawa in 1952 at a polling booth in New York.

Shiko Munakata in Riverside Park, 1959.

Yayoi Kusama, an avant-garde artist, in 1964.

The architect Kenzo Tange on Park Avenue with a sculpture he designed for the Japan Art Festival exhibition in 1966.

A Burmese dancer teaching a Martha Graham dancer, 1975.

Ritual exorcism demonstrated by a member of a Sri Lankan troupe in 1978. (One of the audience asked for a private exorcism.)

The Chhau masked dancers
of Bengal at Carnegie Hall,
1975.

Bugaku (Japanese court music and dance) at Carnegie Hall, 1978. (By mistake, in Texas the poster described it as an "erotic," not "exotic," performance, which may have accounted for the crowds that turned up.)

Bhutanese royal dancers, Carnegie Hall, 1980.

With my mother and Yehudi Menuhin at an Asia Society benefit, 1982.

Left to right: Lukas Foss (composer/conductor), Charles Jones (composer), BSG, Toru Takemitsu (composer) and John Cage (composer) at a Japan Society reception, 1983.

With a Korean shaman dancer (left) and a star of Chinese opera, 1984.

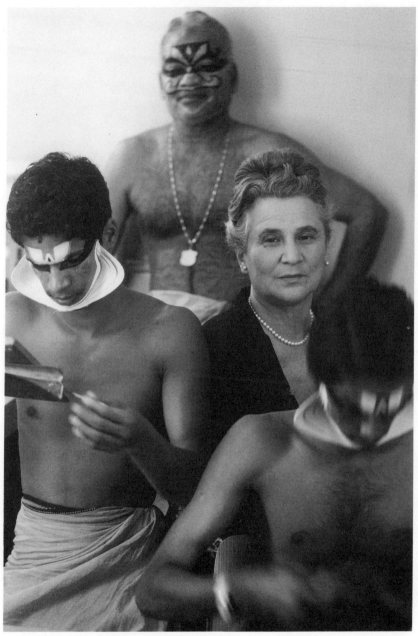

Indian dancers backstage, The Asia Society, 1985.

I was a consultant for Pavarotti's film about China, *Distant Harmonies*.

Career and Family

I could see the small, sturdy figure of Mio-san waving wildly from the dock in Yokohama. Sheilah Hayes, Gen. Whitney's Australian-born secretary, stood there waving too. Sheilah had been billeted with me at the Kanda Kaikan, and we had become close friends. Mio-san kept wiping her eyes with a handkerchief. She must have been calling my name, but I couldn't hear her for the wind. In the glare of the sun, the faces of the crowd below on the pier looked white and already remote.

Standing at the ship's rails, I thought about my visit to Numazu, Mio-san's home town, to deliver food to her family. My father had decided to send them some of the supplies I had obtained for him and my mother through GHQ. So many people crowded into the house in Numazu that day that the floor began to sag. I remembered the weather-beaten face of Mio-san's father, her sisters, with their big eyes just like hers, and the curious villagers, all smiling silently.

Mio-san told me the next day that her family had divided the food equally among the villagers, keeping just a few things for themselves.

"I hope you don't mind," she said. "I know you went to a lot of trouble bringing it down in the jeep. But my father was so pleased he could do something for the village."

Mio-san and Sheilah were still waving as the ship pulled away. Yokohama became smaller and smaller and eventually faded from sight, the horizon nothing but a curve of blue sea. I had been in Japan for a year and a half and had no prospect of returning soon. I realized that if I wanted to see for myself how Japan fared under its new constitution, I would have to look for work in America that would eventually bring me back.

There was someone besides my parents waiting for me in New York. Lt. Joe Gordon had left Japan six months earlier, and we had written to each other regularly. He had attended my father's opening recital at Carnegie Hall and sent a big bouquet backstage, which endeared him to my mother.

Joe was a good-looking man, which I naturally appreciated, but we had a lot in common besides physical attraction—an interest in Japan, in languages, in music and in theater. Most attractive of all was his attitude toward women, whom he instinctively treated as equals.

Joe's knowledge of Japanese was amazing. Having studied the language in military intelligence for only two years, he must have known at least three thousand *kanji* (Chinese characters). I was in awe of this accomplishment. Although my spoken Japanese was better than his, I knew far fewer *kanji*. He had an unusually good ear for music, too. I remember my father hearing Joe whistle and saying in astonishment, "Do you realize, Joe, that you've memorized the development of the whole second movement of a symphony?" His memory never failed to surprise me. Years later, our daughter, Nicky, came home from school one day full of enthusiasm for a book she was reading, Aldous Huxley's *Point Counter Point*. Joe started reciting a page from the book, word for word. I got out Nicky's copy from her schoolbag to check his accuracy— it was perfect.

"How can you remember that?" I asked him. "When did you read it?"

"When I was sixteen."

"But that was thirty-five years ago!" I exclaimed.

Joe was an adventurous person. Why, after all, had he studied Japanese in the first place? He was a New Yorker and had always lived on the East Coast; his life had nothing to do with Asia. Then the war began, and he took a job doing "atomic welding" at a factory in New Jersey. Because of the intense light of the torches, the welders could only work for two-thirds of their eight-hour shifts, resting their eyes for the remainder of the time. Joe and his friend Stanley Amdurer decided to do something constructive in those free hours. They knew they would be drafted soon, and cast about for skills that might prove useful in the army. Plenty of people knew German or Italian, they reasoned, but how many knew Japanese? So they hired a Japanese-American tutor and began studying the language in their breaks at the factory. A few months later, they saw a story in *Life* magazine about a language school for military intelligence officers. They took the test, passed, and began training in the intelligence service. I had never met anyone before Joe who had been able to plan for the future with such accuracy, and I was intrigued. In my own life things had always "just happened."

We were married on January 15, 1948, eight months after I arrived in New York City. He was twenty-nine and I was twenty-four.

My parents were no longer in New York, as my father had been offered a position as artist-in-residence at the St. Louis Institute of Music. He was in high spirits, teaching, performing in the city's concert halls and playing every week on the local radio station, KFUO. He toured other parts of the U.S. as well and even went as far afield as Venezuela. My mother resumed the kind of life she had led in prewar Japan, teaching and socializing. Her trademark Viennese cuisine, enhanced by her years in Japan, helped expand the Sirota social circle.

My parents were granted U.S. citizenship in 1952. Like many other uprooted people, this was something they had hoped for throughout the war years. They never considered going back to Vienna, where vestiges of Nazism remained. Few of our relatives had survived the war in any case, most having died in concentration camps. The handful who did escape had gone to America and England. There was no longer any reason to go back.

Not long after my parents left for St. Louis, Joe and I moved to Pough-keepsie, where he had found a job in the real estate business. Two hours by car from New York City, Poughkeepsie was a quiet, leafy town of about fifty thousand people. The quietness proved deceptive, as the town fairly hummed with social activity, but I never came to enjoy it. The men would all gather on one side of the room and discuss politics, while the women gathered on the other and discussed children, food and fashion. Since I had no children and wasn't terribly interested in food or fashion, I was bored. People were pleasant and well-meaning, but they showed little respect for other people's privacy. Once, a woman I'd met at a cocktail party a few weeks earlier asked me, "Did you wash your cur-tains or are you moving?" I looked at her in astonishment. "I passed your apartment building on Main Street yesterday," she explained. "I noticed your curtains were down, and so I wondered, 'Did she wash her curtains or is she moving?'"

This kind of nosiness got me down.

I started living for the weekend, when our friends from New York came to visit. I would bake Sachertorte on a Thursday, and when Stanley arrived on Friday with his latest girlfriend he would make pitchers of martinis. At seven the next morning Stanley and I, who were both ear-ly risers, would sit down at the kitchen table to a breakfast of leftover martinis and cake, and conduct a postmortem on the previous night's party.

To break the monotony, I began looking for work. Joe was very sup-portive. Since two of his sisters had taken jobs after they were married, he did not feel, as so many American men did at the time, that married women should work only out of absolute financial necessity. Working expanded one's horizons, he thought, and women were as entitled to this experience as men. The problem was finding an employer who shared this enlightened view. I heard of an opening at IBM where I could use my Spanish, but when I wrote "married" on the job application, I was told the company did not hire married women. At a loss about what to do, I spoke to my mother, who advised me to open a dance studio. It seemed like a good idea. I rented a studio and took on fifteen students. But only a few of them were genuinely interested, and fewer still were talented; the others wasted everyone's time talking and fooling about in class. The venture was not a success.

Joe was not very happy selling real estate, either. He had been working toward a master's degree in Far Eastern Studies at Columbia University and found the abrupt transition to the business world difficult. After two years in Poughkeepsie, we gave up suburban life and returned to New York.

Joe resumed his studies, continuing in real estate part-time, and I got a job translating for a bank. The translating was so straightforward I would generally be finished by noon, and found myself killing time in the afternoons reading magazines. Restlessly, I looked around for something more stimulating to do. Then something happened that really intensified my dislike of the bank. One day, seeing a pregnant woman in the staff dining room, the elderly female employee next to me said, "Isn't that disgusting, a pregnant woman working?" I felt as hurt as if the remark had been aimed at me. Could women actually feel such enmity toward other women? Did pregnancy really seem so ugly to them? If so, it would be a long time before women would be able to have families and work happily at the same time. How could we change this male-dominated world if our own perceptions didn't change? I remembered a Japanese saying: "The man who makes his pregnant wife work is not a man"—a comment that originated in an essentially feudal country; but was the status of women in this advanced democracy so very different?

Joe was teaching Japanese at Columbia by this time, and his association with the university soon brought me a more interesting assignment. I was asked to act as the interpreter for the well-known Japanese feminist, Fusae Ichikawa, who was due to arrive in September 1952 as part of a cultural exchange program. The presidential election campaign was at its height, and Miss Ichikawa wanted to observe both the Eisenhower campaign and the women's movement in America.

At fifty-eight, she had the energy, curiosity and appearance of a much younger person. She got up extremely early and, with just enough time for breakfast, was out of the hotel in under an hour, meeting a stream of people until late at night. She used her transit time for naps, falling asleep as soon as she sat down on a bus or a train. The second she arrived she would snap awake, stretch, and announce "I'm ready."

She was the living antithesis of the common American image of Japanese women as timid, wordless creatures, and the talks she gave to women's groups and universities were a series of surprises. I remember the ripple of amazement with which one audience greeted the simple statement that there were women doctors in Japan; clearly, false impressions had not dissipated much since my Mills College days.

I also remember her disappointment at Eleanor Roosevelt's bland response during an interview when she was asked what should be done for the children of GIs and Japanese women born in Japan. "When they grow up," said Mrs. Roosevelt, whose interest in social welfare causes was well known, "they could be given scholarships to American universities."

One day during her visit we had a call from Eisenhower's campaign office in the Commodore Hotel.

"You have an interview tomorrow with the president-elect," his secretary told us.

"But we didn't ask for an interview with him," I blurted out. "We asked for Mamie Eisenhower."

"You have an appointment tomorrow at eleven o'clock," we were coldly informed.

Since Eisenhower was giving no press interviews at the time and no Asian had ever interviewed him before, this—however accidental—was something of a coup. And with only ten minutes allotted to us Miss Ichikawa made the most of it, not hesitating to disagree with him when he urged Japan to take a lesson from the violence in Korea and "look to its own defense." Most Japanese, she pointed out, never wanted to take up arms again, having seen where it got them in the last war.

Eisenhower, who looked more like a jovial businessman than the leader of the nation, gave us double our due time. He even shook my hand at the end, telling me that I was the best interpreter he'd ever had.

"How would he know?" my husband said when I got home. "He doesn't speak a word of Japanese."

Within a year of her return, Miss Ichikawa was elected to the House of Councillors (the upper house of the Japanese Diet) after running a "clean-government" campaign. Her toughness of character was brought home to me again, years later, when I complained to her that I thought bra-burning undignified.

"I know," she said, "but if women in their struggle against inequality have to use shock tactics to get noticed, I'm all for it."

For two months after she left New York, I was at loose ends. Then, in the spring of 1953, I had my first taste of a type of cultural assignment that would become as close to a career as I have ever had. I was invited to work on a special issue of *Theater Arts Magazine* on Japan. Americans in the 1950s knew little, and cared less, about the Japanese arts; there could hardly have been a greater challenge than having to introduce them here.

I knew that the director of the Actor's Studio, Lee Strasberg, was a Kabuki fan and had a collection of photographs of Kabuki actors in their mask-like makeup. This I managed to borrow. I also managed to get an essay on Japanese film from Donald Richie, who was studying at Columbia then and would later become an acknowledged authority. *Rashomon* had won the Grand Prix at the 1951 film festival in Venice, and interest was just picking up.

The success of this enterprise led to a part-time job at the Japan Society. By then, I was pregnant. I knew I wanted to continue working after the baby was born; this wasn't a financial but a personal necessity. Babies certainly require attention, but a mother also needs to maintain a genuine connection with the world outside the home. I realized that hiring a babysitter would cost almost as much as I could earn, but I honestly doubted whether I had the patience to stay with any child all day, even one of my own.

Nicole was born in September 1954 at New York Hospital. Natural childbirth was just beginning to be fashionable in the U.S., and this being the Japanese way, I opted for it. Joe and I took the classes together. Joe tells the story of how when I was in labor I tried not to scream. Japanese women don't scream, so I wasn't going to, either. At one point, though, momentarily overcome by pain, I heard myself cry out.

"How awful. How embarrassing," I said to him. "I screamed."

Just then the doctor walked in, and Joe told him how I had embarrassed myself. The doctor laughed.

"Oh, Beate, that's too bad," he said. "I had this medal I was going to give you." They both laughed till I almost screamed again.

A month later, to my friends' consternation, I entrusted my daughter to a babysitter and started going to work two or three times a week. I would spend a couple of hours away, rush back to nurse Nicole, then go to work again. Joe and I rarely went anywhere socially without toting the baby along in a little collapsible Swiss bed that looked like a suitcase, and she came on all our vacations and trips. Joe was able to spend a good deal of time at home, too, since his work was seasonal. He was actually better with Nicky than I was; my energy failed me when it came to getting up in the middle of the night. For the first three months, till I could bring myself to do it too, he also took care of the diapers, which had to be rinsed in the toilet, put in a container and handed over to the diaper delivery service at the end of the week. It was Joe who deserved that medal.

Meanwhile, my first regular assignment was as a student adviser. The advice I gave was not always good. Our babysitter, for example, who was a Japanese law graduate student studying for an American degree, asked me what I thought about the idea of switching from her present course to modern dance. I asked her how old she was. "Twenty-six," she replied. I told her it was too late, the muscles were no longer elastic enough for the rigors of professional training, and so on. Three years later, she invited me to her graduation performance at Juilliard. When the curtain rose and she stepped out to perform a piece she had choreographed herself, I barely recognized her, and when she danced, it was clear at once that she was very gifted.

In the fifties and sixties, what Japanese students in America had most in common was a shortage of cash. One young violinist I knew whose name is now internationally known was washing dishes. As a musician's daughter, I felt strongly that he should be doing something else with his hands. So, with the help of a small endowment and a title—Director of the Performing Arts Program—I put together teams of young performers who went around to various schools presenting dance and music programs, accompanied by a narrator to explain things. This, I hoped, served not only to give them some useful pocket money but helped foster future audiences with some knowledge of another culture.

At the same time, if a known artist from Japan happened to be coming to the States, I would try to catch him and, with the lure not of money (we didn't have enough) but of access to prestigious halls, make him better known. A case in point was the blind koto player, Kimio Eto. (The koto, a thirteen-stringed zither, was rarely heard outside Japan.) Eto told me that it was his dream to perform with a Western orchestra. Now, I happened to be acquainted with the American composer Henry Cowell, who was interested in Japan. Being young and self-confident, I just rang him up and asked him if he was willing to compose a piece for a visiting koto virtuoso. And he agreed, on condition that I saw that it got performed. He also told me which conductors were interested in his work.

Among them was Leopold Stokowski. I had heard that he had a soft spot for young Japanese women, so I coolly arranged for a bevy of Juilliard students in kimonos to be present at a get-together and to serve him saké, while Eto's music was played over the loudspeaker system. The trap was set ... and the result was that Cowell's concerto, with Eto as the soloist and Stokowski conducting, was played by the Philadelphia Symphony, then went on tour throughout the States.

This episode was my first real lesson in PR, as it is commonly called: the art of manipulating as many people as possible for the sake of publicity. And I became very good at it. PR is, of course, intimately connected with the media. Manipulating the media was behind the success of a display in New York by Sofu Teshigahara, the ikebana master (whose son directed *The Woman in the Dunes*). I wanted Teshigahara's flower arrangement for the lobby of Philharmonic Hall, where a Japanese orchestra would be performing. The lobby was so big, though, that he said he needed a tree. John D. Rockefeller 3rd was president of the Japan Society at the time, and the Rockefeller estate was in Tarrytown, not far away, so I called his secretary and asked for a tree. This I was given. I then decided we needed some publicity. When I walked in and told the editor at the City Desk of *The New York Times* about the cultural event in general, he was unimpressed. "We need a handle," he said. So I told him we were trucking in a Rockefeller tree, and he had his "handle." A photographer was on hand when it arrived and Teshigahara started planting flowers all along it, sticking them in the bark.

In 1958, my son Geoffrey was born, further complicating the delicate career-and-family balancing act I was trying to maintain. Joe, in due course, gave up his academic work, which he excelled at but which didn't pay well enough to be worth continuing. For him the family came first.

In January 1959, a ship arrived bringing another family to New York, one that became a second family for me: the Munakatas.

Shiko Munakata was a woodblock artist who had won the Grand Prix at the Venice Biennale. For a Japanese, he was unusually ebullient and frank, with thick, round glasses and the accent of the far north of his country. He was then fifty-six: his wife, Chiya, was fifty, and their genial-looking son Pariji was twenty-five.

"Thank you for meeting us," Munakata boomed at me. Then: "Do they have salmon in America?"

"You mean the fish?"

"Yes. I love salmon! I have to eat it once a week, to keep my strength up."

His eccentricity extended to the clothes he wore. Usually it was a kimono, but one day I noticed he was wearing a suit that didn't look quite right. Looking more closely, I saw that the right pocket was up high while the left one was low down, and the trouser legs were of different lengths.

"This is the new fashion," he explained. "I asked the tailor to make something especially for *me*—to fit my character, not just my shape."

When he unpacked the prints he'd brought with him for a one-man show at the Willard Gallery, they tumbled out, wrinkled, wrapped in bits of newspaper, the edges bent. The gallery owner looked distraught.

"I thought you'd bring them ready to hang," she said.

"It's better not to confine the prints to frames," she was told. "They're alive—they don't like to be penned in."

To please her, though, since she looked ready to call the whole show off, he produced an iron and quickly pressed them flat.

Snow began to fall on the day he was due to give a lecture/demonstration, and by the afternoon it was a blizzard.

"Don't worry, Beate," he said. "If only one person comes and understands my work, I'll be quite happy."

Luckily, five people came. Munakata, rather than discuss technique, talked about his source of inspiration—Buddhism—saying it wasn't he who did the carving but some greater power; art wasn't ever something you produced by yourself. He then gave a demonstration of how a print was made. He took a thin piece of paper and made a sketch on it before pasting it face-down on the block. Working at astonishing speed, he started to carve through the paper with a chisel. His nose was almost touching the block, his head moving from left to right. Then, just as quickly, he dipped a brush in some black ink and water and spread it over the block. On this he placed a piece of paper dampened to facilitate the transfer of ink and to prevent it from shrinking. First slowly, then very rapidly, he rubbed a bamboo pad over it and, while we held our breath, carefully removed the paper. Finally, he painted some light colors onto the back of the print. When he held up the finished work, the effect was fabulous.

In December 1963, three hundred of my father's former pupils invited him, along with my mother, to return to Japan. They had been away for seventeen years. Leo Sirota played Beethoven, Chopin, Schubert and Liszt, as well as Kosaku Yamada's compositions. For the finale, my father and his pupils played a Bach concerto, after which the audience gave him a standing ovation and almost everybody wept. He told me that the trip had been like a dream from beginning to end. At the age of seventy-seven, he was finally able to put aside his memories of the war years and make his peace with Japan.

"When I can't play the piano any more, I'll be ready to die," he said. On February 24, 1965, with both hands swollen, no longer able to play, he died. He was seventy-nine. A St. Louis paper called him "one of life's unsung heroes, remembered by a multitude of admirers."

My mother moved to New York and took an apartment in our building. She was on the second floor, and we were on the twelfth. Although she kept herself occupied helping us with the children, she was lonely and badly needed companionship. Joe and I discussed this as the problem got worse. Finally we hit on a solution: why not ask Mio-san to come over from Japan? We had kept in touch with her, and I had visited her whenever I went there on business. Mio-san was surprised when we broached the subject in a long-distance phone call, though it was nothing compared with the surprise her husband and two children must have felt.

"My kids are already independent," she said, her voice sounding loud and clear. "I may not know the language, but as long as I'm going to where Beate-san lives, I'm not worried. I would *like* to go to New York."

With her husband's grudging consent she left for America, arriving in New York in 1966, at the age of fifty. Here was a Japanese wife acting like a truly liberated woman. I liked to think it had its roots at least partly in the work I'd done twenty years earlier.

Mio-san wore glasses now, but apart from that she had changed very little. Her energy and openness were just as I remembered. If she disliked something she spoke up, and she wasn't easily daunted. Her cooking was still excellent. In her capable hands, the distinctive cuisine developed by my mother in Kiev, Vienna and Tokyo was soon revived in our house.

My mother poured out her feelings of loneliness and sadness to her new companion. The two of them found that the frictions of the past were no longer a problem; now that Mio-san was older, she knew how to avoid arguments with my temperamental mother, simply saying, "Okay, okay, we'll do it your way." They had always been friends, despite their occasional rows. And to me, an only child, she was like a reliable older sister.

Mio-san went back to Japan in 1970. She had lived with us for two years and worked for the Japanese ambassador to the United Nations for another two, while continuing to help us whenever she had time. She had become a dearly beloved friend and member of the family.

Life seemed to be following a fairly normal course until, at a routine physical examination in 1968, my gynecologist discovered a small lump in my breast. He decided it had to operated on at once. I was upset, especially since I had just received a grant to produce a summer program at The Asia Society that would expose public school children to the various arts of Asia. I had persuaded The Asia Society Gallery, which at that time was not in favor of allowing children near the precious art objects on display, to lend me a few things, which I planned to put on view in the lecture hall. I was going to present two hours of film, music, calligraphy, dance and origami, and the children would be allowed to handle the swords, fans and instruments used by the performers.

I told the surgeon I had to be out of the hospital by a certain date in order to supervise rehearsals.

"Impossible," he said. "Even if you're out of here in time, you'll have to take it easy for several weeks at home."

My gynecologist was more reassuring.

"Don't worry, Beate," he said. "He doesn't know you. You'll be out of the hospital and doing your thing as planned."

The night before the operation, after visiting hours were over and Joe had left, I drank a small bottle of saké that I'd smuggled into the hospital and fell asleep. What I remember most vividly about the whole procedure is waking up in the recovery room and asking for water. Nobody came. There were lots of nurses around, but they were busy with a young woman in critical condition after a lung operation. I tried to make eye contact with someone, anyone, not only to ask for water but to establish that I really was awake and "here," as I fought the lingering effect of the anesthetic. It was a long time before someone came over and gave me some chips of ice. I felt pathetically grateful. If there is a moral here, it is: don't drink saké before an operation.

On my way home five days later, I just "stuck my head" into the lecture hall to see how the lighting had been set up—I couldn't resist.

The "black tie and cocktails" side of my career, which increased when I started doing similar work for The Asia Society from 1960 on, and which I frankly enjoyed (my mother's blood), was something Joe couldn't stand. This wasn't the only difference between us, he being cleverer, more punctual and funnier than I am. His sense of humor, in fact—and the writings of S. J. Perelman—have stood him in good stead through some hard times: the McCarthy era, when close friends were harassed, times when money was tight, and times when death took away people important to us. Several aspects of our relationship are captured in one particular episode. When I first met him in Tokyo, he told me a joke: one person says to the other, "Will you join me in a cup of tea?" The other replies, "Will there be room?" I went to Col. Kades and told him that Lt. Gordon had told me a joke that went like this: one person says to the other, "Will you join me in a teacup?" and the other replies, "Will there be room?" Kades looked baffled. Joe asked me never to repeat a joke of his again.

My increased work load affected our children, too, who as adults now claim I was never at home. This isn't really fair, since until Nicole was fourteen and Geoffrey eleven I never worked full-time. From an early age, I tried to involve them in my job, assigning them small tasks during rehearsals: Nicky ran the stopwatch, timing dances and music, and Geoffrey worked the tape recorder. When they were respectively ten and seven, we took them to the country I'd grown up in, where TBS made a TV film called *Nicky no Nikki* (Nicky's Diary) about these two foreign children's reactions to Japan. This had scenes of them staging a samurai sword fight, with Geoffrey lying in a wounded heap, and him trying to eat some slippery noodles with chopsticks and finally using his hands to stuff them in his mouth.

I had warned him that on Japanese trains in those days one sometimes saw men in their long underwear, with their trousers hung up to keep the crease in them. Boarding a train, he came up with an impromptu poem: "Nobody looks / Nobody cares / Everybody in their underwears."

Besides Japan, both children visited the Soviet Union, where Nicole could use her Russian. She had shown an early interest in the language and by the age of fifteen could speak it fluently. Nicky had always been a responsive student, and had stuck to her piano lessons with her grandmother. Later, she went on to get a degree in classics at Barnard College, then studied law at Columbia, eventually devoting her legal career to public service, working for clean elections. (Drawn also to the arts, she won an Emmy for an educational film dramatizing the ratification of the U.S. Constitution.)

With Geoffrey, however, it was a different story. I tried to make him learn the piano, but he showed no interest in it whatsoever. From kindergarten on, he was inattentive in class, and it was difficult to make him change his mind once he'd decided not to do something. Sometimes, when he let his emotions burst out, he was unmanageable. Joe was not worried, though, and in the end was proved right: Geoffrey graduated summa cum laude, Phi Beta Kappa from Columbia and became a writer and performer, giving me the satisfaction of helping to arrange for his play *Short Change* to be performed in Russian in Khabarovsk, among other cities, after its New York premiere.

When they were still in their teens, for several summers our regular family vacation spot was Mallorca. By the third visit, they were bored; they missed their friends. Then they had a brainwave: why didn't I arrange an introduction to the Beatles through my friend Yoko Ono, who was in London at the time. I was reluctant. The Beatles were at the height of their popularity and constantly badgered by fans. But I called Yoko, who said she'd see what she could do. During dinner with my aunt in London, the phone rang. If we came to the EMI studios right away, Yoko said, the Beatles would be in a recording session and John Lennon would take us in—only the children, though. We grabbed a taxi and rushed over. Looking very pale, Yoko met us at a rear entrance and ushered us in. For two hours while the children were inside, Yoko and I talked in a little anteroom. She told me of the difficulties she was experiencing in England, of the hate mail she was getting, of the hostility of the other Beatles.

I had known Yoko since her days as a student at Sarah Lawrence College. She had been a very pretty and elegant young woman, and I remembered her sitting happily on my living room couch with her fiancé, the composer and pianist Toshi Ichiyanagi. Her well-to-do parents had been strongly opposed to their marriage, refusing to help the young couple in any way.

Yoko and Toshi became disciples of John Cage and started appearing in "happenings." I tried to provide sidelines for them, arranging for Toshi to play the piano in my school programs and Yoko to give demonstrations of calligraphy, origami and the tea ceremony at various functions. Joe had her do a tea ceremony for one of the classes he taught at Queens College, for example. Clad in a kimono, she went through the whole rigmarole, commenting in excellent English on every aspect of it: the steam rising from the kettle, the use of the tea bowls, the need to leave all worldly thoughts behind while contemplating the scroll hanging on the wall and the flower arrangement. She explained why the entrance to the tea room was so low and narrow, saying it was to make sword-bearing guests leave their weapons behind. It was an impressive presentation.

When she had finished, Joe asked the class if there were any questions. There was only one: "Do they take sugar in their tea?" I often wondered whether this incident contributed to Joe's decision to give up teaching.

I also remembered going to Yoko's first "happening." Joe offered to drive me there, but refused to go in. I climbed the rickety stairs of an old wooden loft building. The large room was bare except for a refrigerator, some wooden beer barrels that served as seats, and a handful of spectators, among them a reporter.

Yoko ran to the refrigerator, took out some eggs and, running to a wall covered with a huge piece of white paper, hurled the eggs at it. She then ran back and fetched some jello, which she also threw at the wall. Using her hands as brushes, she splattered some black ink on the paper. As a final touch, she lit a match and set fire to the "painting," at which point, looking at all the wood around us, I told myself, "This serves you right for not listening to Joe—we're all going to die in a Soho loft." Luckily, Yoko had put some fire retardant on the paper, and we escaped a fiery death…

The hours passed quickly as we chatted about these memories. When Nicky and Geoffrey emerged, they were radiant. Not only had they been present at a Beatles recording, but John Lennon had give them a promotional package of records from the new Apple label, and Paul McCartney had given them soft drinks and gum. Heaven!

My daughter Nicole presenting Crown Princess Michiko with a bouquet, Manhattan, 1960.

Nicky and Mio-san at a hut on Mt. Fuji, 1964.

Geoffrey with a brass band performing at Expo '70 in Osaka.

Joe sharing a joke with his grandchild Lara.

The family: three generations.

East and West

In the fifties and sixties, Japan was still regarded in America as a defeated country and its people as cultural inferiors, if not enemies. Asian culture in general was "exotic." Only a handful of scholars understood its richness and variety.

From 1970 on, when I became head of the Performing Arts Program of The Asia Society, I put all my efforts into trying to communicate the essence of Asian culture to Americans through first-rate, purely traditional art forms. To this end, I spent from four to six weeks every year in Asia, researching the old arts and negotiating with the performers, before bringing them to the States. To spare the society's budget, I tried to take in as many countries as possible on each trip.

Adventure was often tempered by discomfort. In Mongolia, I almost froze to death in a yurt. In Tibet, I must have been the only visitor to Lhasa who never got to see the Potala Palace, suffering as I was from the miseries of mountain sickness; all I got for my pains was a performance of "La Paloma" by a seventy-five-piece orchestra and a solo trumpeter. On many of these forays abroad I had to deal with uncooperative bureaucrats, and I learned that cultural exchange with Muslim countries was likely to be complicated by the prevailing attitude toward women. The Iranian government, for example, required a lot of persuasion to allow a woman's voice—that of the Shah's last court singer, Hotere Parvaneh—to be heard in the U.S.

Above all, I learned the value of perseverance.

The puppet theater of Awaji Island, situated in the Inland Sea off the southern coast of mainland Japan, dates back four hundred years. In 1700 there were forty-six troupes; today there is only one.

I had heard about it, but not seen it for myself; I knew it was a folk art with "the smell of the earth" about it, that its puppets were bigger than the more famous puppets of Bunraku, and the narrators were all women. Thinking it might go down well in America, I went to the island in early 1972 to check it out.

When I stepped off the ferry, the mayor and Mr. Umazume, the manager of the theater, were waiting for me. I was given a tour of the island, then a meal where the raw fish was so fresh that the carcass from which the flesh had been cut was still quivering; only by closing my eyes could I get a slice down. The next day, I was shown two puppet plays. Most Western puppets are operated invisibly from above by strings or from below by hands, but these were manipulated entirely by puppeteers on stage. Three of them formed a team: one person handled the head and the right hand, one the left hand, and a third the legs and lower half of the torso. To the accompaniment of a samisen, rhythmic chanting moved the story forward. When the puppet raised its eyebrows, the chanter raised hers; when the puppet wept, the chanter wept. (Later, in America, I saw tears running down the chanter's cheeks at every performance they gave.) My only reservation was about the age of the puppeteers: the oldest was eighty-two and their average age was sixty-five.

"Have you heard of Carnegie Hall?" I asked the mayor and the manager. "What do you think of having the puppets perform there?"

They both looked blank. Thinking they had never heard of it, I started to explain, but Masaru Mori, head of the Awaji Puppet Association, interrupted.

"You mean, the *famous* Carnegie Hall?"

Scrutinizing my business card, he asked me very politely what kind of position "Director of Performing Arts" was and how many people worked for me. Then I understood. In Japan, when a high-ranking person comes to negotiate something, he or she comes with a staff. My being a woman had made them dubious to begin with; the fact that I'd turned up alone made them thoroughly skeptical. It was clear that one round of discussions was not going to be enough. And, not surprisingly, when I visited Awaji again three months later, they were more forthcoming, letting me pick and choose among a number of plays they put on for me.

Over the next two years I worked to raise money for their tour, approaching as many foundations and individual patrons of the arts as I could. Funding was a constant problem for anyone in this line of work, forcing producers to limit the size of troupes, to say nothing of the performers' fees. In January 1974, however, the fourteen-member Awaji troupe finally arrived in New York.

"You're a good woman, Mrs. Gordon, but you're also a tyrant," the manager said as I hurried him over to Carnegie Hall before he could rest after twenty-six hours of travel. Success at Carnegie Hall was a long-held dream of mine. I looked out at the auditorium. White walls, red seats. A ceiling four stories high. Two thousand, seven hundred and sixty seats to fill. Would people come? I could almost hear the buzz of the audience before the curtain went up, the sudden quiet, the roar of applause at the end.

The puppets performed first at Harvard and then at Wesleyan College, to sold-out houses, but the audiences were largely made up of children and students, not sophisticated and hypercritical New Yorkers.

On the day before the Carnegie Hall show, Mr. Mori, head of the Puppet Association, arrived, bringing trouble with him. He said he wanted to give a welcoming speech before the performance; he had even brought along a kimono with his family crest on it for the occasion. When I

explained that it wasn't the practice here to give speeches before professional performances, the puppeteers objected; they wouldn't go on if he
wasn't allowed to speak. I appealed to the people at The Asia Society,
explaining that in Japan a speech by the representative of a traditional
arts troupe was customary, was considered part of the performance.

"In that case, just thirty seconds," I was told.

"Make it a minute, since it'll have to be translated," I said.

On the big day, the troupe wanted to make their stage preparations
well in advance, but the union stagehands said very firmly this couldn't
be done before 2:00 P.M. The puppeteers were upset. They blamed me.
Then at two o'clock the stagehands interfered again.

"Anything on stage is our work," they said. "Just tell us what you want
done and we'll do it."

For the Awaji people, who not only made their own implements and
props but usually swept the stage floor themselves, it was a huge inconve-
nience to have to tell others through an interpreter to hammer in a nail
for them. Still, this was America, and work was carried out according to
union rules.

It started to snow early in the evening.

"People won't come," the manager fretted.

Fifteen minutes before the curtain, there were only three people, all
Japanese, in the audience. Five minutes later, there were a hundred. I
was wringing my hands. Two and a half years of arduous preparation—for
this? With five minutes to go, people who had apparently been waiting in
the lobby for friends came streaming in from all sides. When the bell
rang, the orchestra seats were packed, mostly with Americans. Manage-
ment said there were one thousand, eight hundred people in the audience. We did it, I told myself.

The next day, the hall was full again. From the hall manager down to
the doormen, the attitude at Carnegie Hall became friendlier. And with a
two-night audience of some three thousand, six hundred people, The Asia
Society had set a new record for itself.

Just one unfortunate incident threatened to spoil things. After the last show, the bus carrying their equipment back to the hotel stopped somewhere in Harlem to get some gas, and while the driver was talking to the attendant, someone stole two of the boxes. A puppet horse's head and a male puppet's body were in them.

Those puppets are very old, and irreplaceable. I went on television to ask for their return. Two days later an anonymous call led us to a yard where the remains of the puppets lay, covered in mud and drenched with rain. They were unusable. But word had spread about the incident, expressions of sympathy poured in, and tickets were sold out in Washington and other upcoming venues. Not for the first time, I learned the wisdom of not losing hope too quickly.

When I told people I wanted to see traditional Asian arts, I was often shown new arrangements of them, either because they thought I would prefer them that way or because they were trying to conform to what they considered Western standards. On such occasions, I would use Japan as a model to explain what I wanted. In Japan, I told them, Kabuki and No theater are preserved strictly according to the old style of doing them, and they are flourishing, alongside other, modern forms of entertainment. What is important, I pointed out, is to avoid mixing old and new haphazardly, spoiling both of them.

In Burma one year, after making laborious arrangements to attend a national festival, I was confronted with versions of classical Burmese dances that had obviously been influenced by a popular all-girl Japanese revue which is notorious for the level of flashy kitsch it manages to attain. As a producer, I felt let down, and wandered disconsolately through the streets of Rangoon that night. Cities in the tropics come alive at night, and Rangoon throbbed to the sound of American pop music performed by local groups. It didn't bode well. But then, walking again the next morning, I suddenly heard the rhythmic sound of wooden clappers. When I asked my interpreter what it was, he said it came from a school of dance nearby. I asked to see the school. We entered a ramshackle building. To the beat of the clappers worked by an old woman, a group of ten girls was going through some of the 104 time-honored exercises of classical dance (boys do 103). Watching their fluid, intricate movements, I thought: this is it. They reminded me of Martha Graham's famous exercises in their formal presentation.

After overcoming the objections of Burmese officials, who could not understand why I wanted to present mere "exercises" to American audiences, and after adding a few actual dances to the program, I left them to prepare for their visit to New York.

Several months later I flew back to see rehearsals and, in particular, costumes. It was a shock. Instead of the unobtrusive movements and plain cotton sarongs I'd seen before, it was all velvet and silk and pearls, and girls dancing with boys. I put my foot down. "But the choreography's classical," I was told, "—from 1942."

Persuaded to resurrect the original costumes and format, they went on to an enthusiastic reception in New York. Martha Graham saw them and invited them to perform at a party in her studio. The elite of the dance world was there. The Burmese in their simple earth-colored sarongs gave an impression simultaneously of great suppleness and great dignity as they changed position seamlessly, one movement flowing into the next, never seeming to strain or lose breath, however demanding the move. They were followed by the large and powerful Graham dancers in flesh-colored leotards. Although they performed their exercises expertly, you could hear them breathing, and their bodies ran with sweat. It was a display of aggressive physicality.

One of the spectators came over to me afterward and said: "You know what the difference is between East and West?"

"No."

"It's sweat."

In August 1973, when the Vietnam War looked as if it might at last be coming to an end, I traveled to the village of Purulia in West Bengal to see the dances of the Chhau.

Indian dance has four classical styles—Kathak and Manipuri in the north, Bharata Natyam and Kathakali in the south—but Chhau is a separate form, a ritual folk dance performed to bring rain to the fields.

I was met in Calcutta by Dr. Battacharya, a professor of anthropology, who traveled with me. It was a trip of only 185 miles, but it took us a day and a half to get there by car as we were caught in a monsoon and had to stop overnight en route. We reached Purulia toward evening, where we were put up in one of several bungalows left over from British colonial times; a bare wooden hut with, surprisingly, a flush toilet.

The village lay deep in the Bengali forest. I remember thinking that the darkness of the distant past must have been like this. One felt completely enclosed by it. Peering into the night, I could see nothing, but was aware of all kinds of sounds and movements: animals, birds ... and then, faintly at first, the boom and thud of what seemed to be drums. It was like being caught in a dream.

As it turned out, I *was* dreaming, but it was a dream that shaded into reality. Since we'd arrived later than expected, the Chhau had got tired of waiting and gone back to their huts in the hills. Dr. Battacharya had sent runners to bring them back, but I had fallen asleep waiting for them, and it was the drumming that woke me up.

We went outside. It was 2:00 A.M. The sound of drums and shawms came closer, there was the flicker of torches, and into the clearing came forty people carrying ladders to which great masks crowned with beads and feathers were attached. And in the torchlight there at the dead of night they danced their masked dances for us, at first slowly, then whirling wildly and leaping in their black-and-white striped robes. They were fantastic.

After watching for several hours, I decided to invite eleven of them to the States. Everyone was paid two dollars for having come. Then I went back to my room. An hour later, though, I could still hear voices from my companion's room. Thinking something must be wrong, I went to investigate.

"I'm asking each of them for a receipt for the money," he explained.

"But I don't need that," I assured him.

"*I* am the one who needs the receipts. I don't want the local politicians accusing me of favoritism. I want to be able to show them that we treated everyone fairly and paid them all the same amount, and that the choice of performers was completely up to you. They can't read or write, so I've got an ink pad for their thumbprints."

The next day, Dr. Battacharya seemed relaxed.

"Don't worry," he said, "I'll see that the people you've chosen don't die before they get there." It was a reasonable reassurance to offer. Bengal was experiencing a serious famine that year, and everywhere I looked, people, cows and dogs appeared emaciated. In a climate where the temperature can exceed 110°, and where people have to cope with overpowering natural forces, death is always close at hand.

On the way back to Calcutta, the driver of the rented car in which Dr. Battachaya, a student of his, and I were riding was going too fast. I asked him to slow down, but he didn't listen. All at once I was thrown forward as we lurched to a stop. We had hit a man on a bicycle. The rider's body had slammed into the windshield, then fallen to the ground, where it lay near the broken bicycle. To my horror, the driver did not get out but immediately drove off at high speed. Pieces of glass from the windshield flew back into my face, which I had to cover with a sweater. I kept asking why we didn't turn back.

"If he'd stopped the car there," the professor explained, "the village people would have killed him."

"But what about the man who was hurt?"

There was no reply. The car sped on. Frantically, I insisted we go back, but we only went faster still. Then, twenty miles further on, two policemen standing in the middle of the road with walkie-talkies flagged us down. The driver was arrested. I was supposed to take a plane to Sri Lanka that day, and when I told the police, they let the rest of us continue our journey by bus.

At the airport, I begged Dr. Battacharya to call the village and ask how the injured man was doing. He was alive, but in serious condition. I told the professor I wanted to give his family some money for medical expenses. At this, the student burst out:

"Don't worry about him so much! He's a middle-aged man, and probably nothing *can* be done for him. But the driver is young, and will go to jail, and he has a wife and children. *He* is the one who needs help."

Eighteen months later, in 1975, the Chhau troupe's tour took place with Dr. Battacharya acting as their chaperon. I was keen to show the visitors some of the wonders of New York—the Empire State Building, a Broadway musical—before they started.

"That isn't necessary," the professor advised me. "Leave them at the hotel, where they can watch television, eat and sleep. That's all they need."

I thought this was unkind; he seemed to be speaking from the standpoint of his Brahmin caste. So I had them taken to the Empire State anyway. Looking suspiciously at the elevator, they refused to enter. "We are not getting into this box," declared one, and the others instantly agreed. When their guide suggested going somewhere else, they asked to be taken back to the hotel. They wanted to watch television, eat and sleep.

At Carnegie Hall, they were a sensation. Rain actually fell on Manhattan when they did the rain dance.

At the end of their six-week tour, I gave them a check for the fee I owed them. As a separate gift they could use for shopping, I gave them forty dollars each in cash. But when they opened the envelopes, they threw the money at me. "We work for six weeks and you only pay us forty dollars!" they yelled.

Embarrassed, Dr. Battacharya tried to explain to them, but never having seen a check before, they didn't believe a word he said. I was flustered and miserable, close to tears.

"They're like children," he said. "They'll have forgotten all about it by tomorrow. And just as he'd predicted, after he had taken them to the bank and cashed the check, they were all smiles when they came to say goodbye—they actually kissed my feet! They were weighed down with flashlights, transistor radios and even bicycles.

Following the widely reported success of these dancers in the U.S., an article appeared in a British magazine questioning the wisdom of taking people from an underdeveloped area and immersing them in American culture. How could they fit in to their own society again after such an experience? I told Dr. Battacharya about the article when I met him again years later.

"The flashlights and radios they bought were put away in a corner when the batteries ran out," he said. "The bicycles' tires soon got punctured. Within a few months, they all recovered from whatever culture shock they'd undergone and returned completely to their old way of life."

After 1976, the pace of work at The Asia Society accelerated rapidly. Among the more unusual performers we brought to America during this period were the great Indian dancer Sitara Devi and the Qawwali singers from Pakistan.

Sitara was a fiery personality who didn't take kindly to any kind of criticism. I once questioned the authenticity of her costumes, which were very showy, with hundreds of sequins on them. Why couldn't she wear her beautiful Benares saris? Because they wouldn't show up on the stage, she said. I complained that it made her look like a nightclub act. She was furious.

"You want authentic?" she shouted. "You want really authentic? Then I'll go topless! *That's* authentic."

Two days before her debut at Carnegie Hall, she developed a fever and backache. I called my doctor, begging him to make a house call. After examining her at her hotel, he told me she was coming down with pneumonia, and that he would prescribe an antibiotic and try to get her fever down. I said I would cancel the performance; we couldn't jeopardize her health.

"Are you kidding?" he laughed. "That woman would dance even if you stood on your head begging her not to! Did you see those muscles in her legs? They're made of iron!"

The doctor was right. Sitara danced—danced brilliantly.

A week later, in the Midwest, a party was given in her honor. Her brother, a drummer given to drink, was usually kept on a short leash by her. But someone forgot to watch him, and before long he was weaving around muttering "She thinks she's so great, without me she's nothing!"

Without saying a word, Sitara took off a high-heeled shoe, hit him hard on the head with it and walked away. We lugged him out and had him taken to his hotel. Quite unconcerned, Sitara went on entertaining the party for another six hours.

With the Qawwali singers I had some of the same problems and some quite new. There was the familiar disagreement about dress. Along with their white tunics and fur hats, they wore large, shiny gold watches. When asked to remove them, they were astonished. "But this is good, this is beautiful," they said. If I didn't appreciate them, it showed a lack of taste on *my* part, not theirs.

A rather more significant problem arose in the course of their actual performance. One of the characteristic features of their strange and wonderful music is the rapturous atmosphere it produces. This had the effect of driving some of the Pakistanis in the audience up to the stage, where they tossed money at the musicians. One man beat his head in ecstasy against the stage until he bled and had to be carried out. Carnegie Hall had never seen anything like it.

Another year I visited Sarawak. I was the guest of an elderly couple in a tribe of former headhunters, staying in a longhouse after a journey by helicopter and speedboat. The woman, tattooed all over from her feet to her hips, and wearing earrings that pulled her earlobes down past her shoulders, was fond of cigars. Headhunting had been outlawed since 1962, but as my husband said, "How would they know about the law? They can't read." So when the old chief asked me to dance, I danced, feeling ridiculous in a feather headdress.

To my amazement, later, while I lay on the hard floor with everybody else, waiting for sleep, the man lying next to me spoke to me in English. He said he was an anthropologist from Kuala Lumpur and was conducting a survey of the jungle people who had been forced out of their habitat by commercial logging. He had been to the United States, he said.

"Whereabouts?" I asked.

"You wouldn't know. It's a little place on the East Coast where many Ukrainians live."

"What's it called?"

"Kerhonkson," he said.

I burst out laughing.

"That's where my husband is dealing in real estate!"

My mother died in 1985 at the age of ninety-one. She had recovered from breast cancer surgery, but succumbed to the quieter ravages of age. To the day she died, she continued to take pride in her appearance. She had helped us a great deal when the children were small, and had been a loyal fan of my activities. With the rest of the family she came to almost all the shows I produced, although her admiration for the arts of Asia never replaced her love of Western culture. I shall never forget her wistfully remarking, after seeing hundreds of my concerts, "Beate, can't you bring something from Paris?"

I myself finally retired from The Asia Society in 1993 at the age of sixty-nine, after twenty-three years of hard work. My father performed in public until the age of seventy-nine, so I hope to keep going for as long as he did. I have a dream still: of taking the best of international performing arts and creating a "caravan" that would tour the great cities of the world.

I have enjoyed the work. I believe that work enjoyed is one of the greatest satisfactions life can provide. I have also believed *in* this work. "Cultural exchange" is a dry, official-sounding term, as remote from most people as the U.N. with its ear-phoned faces behind cards with the names of different countries on them. I have tried to make it less remote. Not to dilute it, not to make it "more like us," but to bring the strangeness closer so that we can see it, touch it, hear it clear its throat and sing. Art shouldn't be difficult. Learning shouldn't be solemn. Culture shouldn't be forbidding.

Through my work, I have come to hold one other firm belief: that, in time, women can and must play an equal role with men. There should be no need for their influence to be limited, to be wielded as it was in my experience, by the only woman in the room.